WHY I SLEPT WITH MY THERAPIST

How One Gay Man Tried to Go Straight

BRIAN ANTHONY KRAEMER

iUniverse, Inc.
Bloomington

Why I Slept with My Therapist
How One Gay Man Tried to Go Straight

Copyright © 2011 Brian Anthony Kraemer

All rights reserved. No part of this book may be used or reproduced by any means, graphic, electronic, or mechanical, including photocopying, recording, taping or by any information storage retrieval system without the written permission of the publisher except in the case of brief quotations embodied in critical articles and reviews.

iUniverse books may be ordered through booksellers or by contacting:

iUniverse
1663 Liberty Drive
Bloomington, IN 47403
www.iuniverse.com
1-800-Authors (1-800-288-4677)

Because of the dynamic nature of the Internet, any Web addresses or links contained in this book may have changed since publication and may no longer be valid. The views expressed in this work are solely those of the author and do not necessarily reflect the views of the publisher, and the publisher hereby disclaims any responsibility for them.

Any people depicted in stock imagery provided by Thinkstock are models, and such images are being used for illustrative purposes only.

Certain stock imagery © Thinkstock.

ISBN: 978-1-4620-6720-6 (sc)
ISBN: 978-1-4620-6721-3 (hc)
ISBN: 978-1-4620-6722-0 (e)

Library of Congress Control Number: 2011960418

Printed in the United States of America

iUniverse rev. date: 11/16/2011

Contents

Prologue vii
A Change of Plans 1
Set Ablaze 4
Demons 6
Thirteen Years of Celibacy 10
Time for a Therapist 12
Spiritual Grandpa 15
In His Arms 17
Anxiety and Depression 20
May I Call You Dad? 22
Sexually Aroused 24
Many Intimate Friends 27
It's Working! 30
Early Sessions 32
Accused 34
Could I Have Done It? 38
Letters to My Parents 40
Penis Size and Underwear Brand 42
Going Home for the First Time 44
I Feel Sick Inside 48
Hooked Up to a Polygraph Machine 51
Preparing for the Weekend with Tim 55
Crossing the Line 59

Why Did He Do It? 62

James Confesses He Lied 66

Overnight at Tim's New House and the Cabin. 70

Dissociative Alter Egos or Childish
Role-Playing? 73

More Counseling Sessions 79

Three Men and a Boy in a Bed 81

It's Not Working 84

Working with a Female Therapist 92

Time to File a Complaint 94

Heat of Summer 97

Nature Speaks Again 100

A Cold Winter 102

A New Life 106

New Freedoms 109

Marriage, Massage, and Self-Acceptance . . . 111

End of Therapy, Mission Work, and
Tim's License 114

Resolution 116

Reparative Therapy in the News 118

Epilogue 123

References 125

Prologue

I never intended to write this book. When I began collecting every letter, e-mail, instant message, note, check stub, and journal entry, it was with one goal: to document my innovative and courageous relationship with my therapist, my "father figure" who was going to lead me into a successful transition from gay to straight. I wanted to document and share the details of my sexual and emotional healing.

After thirteen years of celibacy, thousands of pages read on how to go from homosexuality to heterosexuality, counseling, daily prayer, and two exorcisms, I was intent on becoming straight. I was convinced it was sinful to be gay, and if acted upon, being gay would result in my spending an eternity in a burning fiery hell, separated from everyone and everything I loved and from everyone who loved me. It was following these thirteen years of celibacy that I consulted with the therapist with whom I built the father-son relationship detailed here.

In those years, I read many times that my homosexual desires were the result of a faulty relationship with my parents in early childhood. According to Dr. Joseph Nicolosi (1991), author of *Reparative Therapy of Male Homosexuality*, I had failed to identify with my father's masculinity and had instead identified with my mother's femininity. According to the theory, the mothers of homosexual boys are most often domineering and overbearing, and their fathers are passive and uninvolved, so lacking an internal sense of my own masculinity, I looked for it outside of myself and thus longed for intimacy with men. What I needed was to "to repair the original gender-identity injury" (1991, p. xvi) by working with a caring male therapist with whom I built an intimate but nonsexual bond, something Dr. Nicolosi refers to as a "reparenting process" (1991, p. 180). "In relationship with a same-sex therapist, a client can find some of what he missed in the failed father-son bond" (1991, p. 150). I could reclaim my lost male self. Nicolosi (1993) also writes that homosexual men have a "hurting little boy" (p. 54) inside who needs to be comforted and healed by intimate, but nonsexual, male relationships. He gives a positive example (1993, p. 62) of a gay man finding emotional healing in being held in the arms of a heterosexual man. Speaking of the therapeutic relationship, he says, "The therapist must be the 'good enough' father, willing to be 'for' the son. He must reach out and give of himself sincerely and compassionately. He must challenge the client in a way that is direct and honest, without manipulating or contaminating the relationship with his own needs" (1991, p. 182).

My therapist took these ideas to a new level. With a handful of his clients, including me, he felt that God had called him to "spiritually adopt" us. I was so happy and hopeful from the beginning of our relationship that I wanted to document the success of this innovative approach to sexual healing and had already decided on the title of a book—*May I Call You Dad?*—that would detail it.

That book was never written; instead, this present one needed to be. The file of materials I collected throughout our relationship that was intended to document my conversion from gay to straight became a dossier that authorities used to force my therapist to surrender his license for unprofessional conduct.

I wrote this book because I wanted to make sense of the early childhood experiences that left me feeling frightened, lonely, and desperate for physical affection. I want to show how a reparative therapeutic model of homosexuality is harmful to the family because it makes homosexuality an illness and then blames the parents. I want to illustrate how damaging the belief is that being gay or lesbian is sinful and can be, and should be, changed. I want to show how that belief confused my understanding of my feelings and complicated and slowed my efforts to find wholeness. I want to show how my therapist's sexual identity issues clouded his judgment as a professional and how both of us deceived ourselves in our relationship. I want to share my story so that others might know they are not alone.

1

A Change of Plans

Just before Christmas of 1997, I flew from Southern California, where I worked in a Christian mission agency, to visit my parents five hundred miles north. I originally planned to stay for two weeks, from December 20 through January 3, but after a few days, I knew I could not stay that long. I felt anxious, nervous, and afraid. I had to get back to my own home, my gym, and my routine. I was addicted to my daily trips to swim at a local university pool, where I spent long periods of time in the men's locker room showering, hoping to see as many naked men as possible.

I watched men come and go in this group shower setting and tried to avoid being too obvious in my sexual interests. My penis, however, often revealed my thoughts, and I had to direct my erection toward the shower wall and pretend nothing unusual was happening. Most men ignored it. Some engaged in friendly conversation without mentioning it. Others revealed interest with eye contact or by moving closer, to a shower head near mine. Still others gave a scowl of disapproval and left.

With my eyes, I soaked in these masculine bodies in an effort to satiate my longing for any kind of connection with them. Occasionally, one invited me to touch him or made an effort to touch me, but I would refuse his offer and whisper that I was interested only in looking. I could not touch or be touched. I had not had sex with a man since my conversion to Christianity thirteen years before, in May 1984, at age twenty. I wasn't about to break my record of celibacy.

Now, in my parents' home, I felt terribly alone and frightened. I did not want them to see the level of my anxiety. I did not want to tell them that I craved male energy, male attention, if only a fleeting glimpse of a naked man in a public shower room. Not wanting to be rude or abrupt, I asked whether they would mind if I changed my departure date. They protested but also knew that I was determined. I called United Airlines, paid an extra hundred dollars, and changed my flight to December 29, five days earlier than originally scheduled. I felt relieved knowing it would be only a few days before I could leave.

I grew up in this home in a Northern California farming community from age ten to seventeen. I left angry and with resentment toward my mother, with whom I never seemed to get along. After moving out, I attended California State University, Chico, and earned a bachelor's degree in psychology in 1985, a second bachelor's in health science in 1989, and an elementary teaching credential in 1992. I taught for two years in a Christian school and then moved to Southern California to work in a mission agency in September 1994. I usually visited my parents twice a year.

The day before my departure during that Christmas visit, I rose earlier than my parents and went into their living room. With a large front window facing east, and because of the cold in Northern California during the winter, it was nice to open the blinds and let in the morning sun. As I sat in front of the wood fire stove, my mother came in and asked angrily, "Who put these blinds up?" I knew that if I were to confess at that moment, I would come across like a shamed child, eyes down, embarrassed for doing something that had upset her. So I responded in a controlled manner and simply acknowledged the problem. "You didn't want them like that?"

"I bet your father did it," she said, angry and incredulous.

Because I wasn't interested in shaming him any more than myself, I repeated, "You didn't want them like that," this time without the questioning tone, but simply acknowledging the fact.

"Don't talk to me like that!" she said angrily. "When I ask you a question, just give me an answer!"

With matching ferocity, I snapped back, "Listen here. It is just as likely that if I left those blinds down, you would have come in here and said, 'Who left these blinds down?' I don't know how to please you. I can't figure you out."

She instantly broke into tears and declared, "You better watch how you talk to me. You're the Christian one." With that she marched out of the room and to her bedroom, where she likely cried and felt abused and ashamed for setting the brief argument in motion and confused about how it had happened. I felt sad for her, thinking she likely felt guilty and imagined I must hate every minute of my visit because of my defensiveness toward her.

The next day, she and my dad drove me to the airport. It was a sad way to leave, four days after Christmas and two days before New Year's Eve, when my extended family would celebrate together at the home of an uncle and aunt. There was still tension between my mother and me, but we were able to carry on pleasant conversation as we made our way to the airport.

That evening, having arrived back at my rented home in Southern California, I told a Christian friend of mine, Dennis Prince[1], how much I resented my mom, even to the point of tears. He suggested that perhaps God was calling me to move back in with my parents in order to bring healing to our relationship. I told him, "If I were a wolf, I would growl at you over that suggestion." In response to my quip about growling, he encouraged me to be prayed over by a spiritual warfare group because he was concerned I might have demons of hatred, resentment, and homosexuality. When I spoke to my closest friend, Wade Brooks, about it later, I explained, "This isn't the kind of problem one just casts out. Wade, I'm sorry to be so graphic, but my uncle was sucking on my penis when I was nine years old. You don't just pray and cast this kind of thing out."

---

[1] The names of many people, organizations, and places throughout the book have been changed.

2

Set Ablaze

When I was eight or nine, my uncle Robby, my mother's brother, invited me to play with him in my grandparents' home. He was five and a half years older than I. Before these experiences, I was a happy child with a clear conscience and a ready and easy smile. I loved school with its opportunities to read, write, add, subtract, make things with clay, and draw things with crayons. I loved jumping rope with the girls and playing kickball and dodgeball for physical education. I do not remember sadness or fear or anxiety before my sexual encounters with my uncle.

While I was at his home, he invited me to his bedroom. We lay in his bed together, and he rubbed against my body until I felt wetness on my skin. He dried me off with a towel. One time, before he did it, I asked him, "Are you peeing on me?" He walked over to a cot inside his room, sat back on it, his pants and underwear down to his ankles, and began to stroke his penis until a white, gooey stuff came out. I thought it was gross.

These sexual encounters with my uncle were times of guilt-ridden pleasure, creating severe emotional conflicts. I feared getting caught, but each time there was opportunity, I wanted to be with him again. What he had started, I was anxious to continue. One time, Robby and I stood inside the front door of his home beneath a small half-moon glass window. We pulled our pants and underwear down to our ankles, and he lifted me against his erection. I was impressed with the size of his penis. I liked being held against him. He looked through the window again and again to make sure no one was coming.

Though I wasn't forced to engage in these sexual behaviors with my uncle,

I also did not choose them in any meaningful sense of the word. He was older, taller, stronger, and more powerful. He had been introduced to sex by someone older, and he repeated the behavior with me. By nine years old, I had formed a powerful link between the adult male body and sexual pleasure.

During this time, my parents were unaware of what I was doing. Because of this secret, I felt terribly isolated from my parents, utterly alone, and desperately frightened, incapable of feeling safe or close to them or secure in their love. With difficulty, I tried to look them in the eyes when they asked me how I was, but I felt frightened, sad, and guilty. My hands felt dirty, and though I washed them repeatedly, I could not make them feel clean. I developed fears of being evil against my will, of losing my mind, and of dying. I had repeated nightmares.

Throughout this time, I longed to be held by my father, to feel safe and secure in his arms, but he was not a physically affectionate person, and holding or hugging was not something he initiated. I was afraid to ask to be held because I feared he might say no. It was better to believe that he might say yes than to ask and be rejected. That would destroy me. I already feared losing my mind, and I knew his rejection would do it. I also feared he might find the thought of holding me nasty or repulsive, two things I already felt at this young age.

My sexual experiences with my uncle continued for more than a year, until he and my grandparents moved to Fort Bragg in June 1973. By this time, I had acted out my sexual desires with three neighbor boys, one my age, nine; another, eleven; and the third, fourteen. No one knew that by age nine, I was obsessed with sexual pleasure and washed my hands compulsively in an effort to make them feel clean; I was a perfect boy in church and school, yet I was ever tormented with fears of death, evil, hell, and separation from my family.

At age eleven, I told my father I thought I might be gay. He told me I was too young to know and not to worry about it.

3

Demons

My friend's suggestion following my Christmas 1997 visit to my parents that I should consider being prayed over to exorcise demons of hatred, resentment, and homosexuality was not an odd or unfamiliar idea. I had been raised Roman Catholic and was taught that Satan and demons existed and were to be resisted. As early as age nine, the same time I was struggling with guilt over my sexual activities, I feared that demons might be trying to harm me.

One day during childhood, while alone in the house, I sat at the piano playing the song "My Bonnie Lies over the Ocean." I believed there were demons around our home, and they were trying to come into the house and get me, but they hated music. I played and sang the song again and again to keep them outside. I didn't realize it at the time, but I was beginning to experience symptoms of obsessive-compulsive disorder. If I rested my hand on my knee, the thought would come to mind that I needed to do it three times to make sure none of us three kids would die. Sometimes I repeated behaviors five times to accommodate our whole family and six times to protect some other "part" of myself that seemed evil and that was desperately afraid of being left alone.

While I was practicing piano, the thought came to my mind that the phone was about to ring, and unless I was out of the present measure of music before it rang, someone in our family would die, and it would be my fault. The thought came again and again, and no matter how many times I allowed it to frighten me and then breathed a sigh of relief when the phone didn't ring,

I still couldn't stop its return. I began to suspect that perhaps demons were putting these thoughts in my mind in order to torment me. I also focused my attention on some aspect of my bodily functions, such as eye blinking, swallowing, spitting, heart beating, or breathing, or being able to see my nose, and couldn't stop thinking about it. The worst fear was that I was somehow destined for evil, even against my own will, and that eventually it would be revealed that I was a liar and a deceiver and destined for an eternity in hell.

At age eighteen, in my first year at California State University, Chico, I rejected my Roman Catholic faith and became an atheist. I felt liberated, free from a lifetime of religious fears of evil, of disappointing God, and of demons seeking to torment me. I was no longer subject to a prewritten script of how I should live my life. I had believed for years that I was gay but could never act on it because I was Roman Catholic. Now I was free to pursue my sexual desires and longings for intimacy with men.

During the next three years, I had three homosexual relationships that were sexually exciting but that couldn't meet my insatiable longing for connection. I could never feel close enough. It was as if my "love bucket" had holes in it and could not retain the love I received.

As I contemplated a universe created not by a loving, conscious being with purpose and meaning, but by evolution with its random and accidental processes, I felt alone. I longed for intimacy, and a nonthinking universe could not provide it. Other human beings couldn't either. My identity as atheist was replaced with agnostic. I took an Eastern religions class studying Hinduism, Buddhism, and Taoism, while studying Christianity on my own. At the same time, I cried out to the universe and said, "If there is a god out there, I want to know you."

During the next two years, I read *Why I Am Not a Christian*, by Bertrand Russell; *Mere Christianity*, by C. S. Lewis; and *Evidence That Demands a Verdict*, by Josh McDowell. I debated Christians and insisted on logical answers to difficult questions. I became more and more convinced that Christianity was rooted in historical facts but could not reconcile my being gay with my developing confidence in the Christian faith.

As a psychology major, I believed people created their ideas of God from the need for a father figure, yet one of the authors I was reading, psychiatrist Dr. Scott Peck, had become a Christian in his early forties. The late conversion of this intelligent and well-educated man was the catalyst that led to my own conversion. In his book *People of the Lie: The Hope for Healing Human Evil*, he described clients who he believed were possessed by demons and said he observed them writhe like snakes, hissing and cursing with evil voices coming out of their bodies.

Dr. Peck's description of demon possession had an impact on me. I thought, if evil existed, and I had come to believe it did, certainly good existed, and I wanted to be on the side of good. I was told by Christians that one either served God or served Satan, and serving oneself was fine with Satan. I didn't want to be evil. I prayed to give my life to Jesus in May 1984 at age twenty. I said to God, "I don't know if you want me to stop being gay, but if you do, you're going to have to do it in me because I don't really want to, and I don't know how." A little over a month later, I was convinced I could no longer be gay, and I resolved to live out a heterosexual lifestyle.

My first personal experience with exorcism was during the summer of 1989 as a missionary in Tonalá, Mexico. I worked with the pastor and missionary there named Rodolfo Diaz. After I told him about my early childhood sexual experiences and my years of fears and anxiety and having homosexual temptations, he asked if I would like to be prayed over. I said yes, and he attempted to command any demons that might be present to reveal themselves and to leave. In spite of fervent prayer, nothing happened, which I found to be a relief. I did not want to go through the horror of an exorcism.

From 1989 to 1992, I worked as a substitute teacher; I earned my teaching credential in 1992 and taught third and fourth grades in a Christian school until 1994, when I moved to Southern California to work full-time in a mission agency there. In the spring of 1997, I was still concerned that my chronic anxiety and fears might be explainable by demonic oppression or even possession. I sought the help of Larry Myer-Stevens, a counselor who specialized in identifying and casting out demons as part of his therapy. I was afraid that I might be deceiving myself and deceiving others, that I might not really be a Christian and instead might be destined for hell. I had recently accepted masturbation as a normal part of my life after years of struggling with it, but I feared that maybe I was also deceiving myself in this. I didn't feel "saved" or have the assurance that other Christians seemed to have. I talked about my fears incessantly with my Christian friends.

In my application for meeting with Larry, I wrote, "What I really want is to just be held forever by a man, nothing else, not just any man, but a fatherly type man, a masculine man who has a father's heart, a nurturing, forgiving type man, one who has strength, power, calmness, and mercy. I'm beginning to cry as I type this. This image is so powerful for me."

I met with Larry for several sessions, relating my story, before he asked if I would participate in an attempt to identify and cast out demons. With anxiety, but hope for healing, I agreed. The tension of the moment gave me conflicting feelings of nervousness and giddiness as he began to command any demons present to reveal themselves. I watched myself participate in an exorcism, and it struck me as both nerve-wracking and funny.

When fifteen or twenty minutes had passed, and nothing seemed to be happening, I thought it would be funny to say, "I'm not coming out," as if I were a demon. I didn't say it because I knew that if I did, it would greatly confuse the situation. But then out of fear that my thoughts possibly were evidence of real demons, I confessed to Larry that this thought had entered my mind. He did not seem concerned, and our lengthy prayer time came to a conclusion with no apparent demons present. Again, I was glad to be spared a true exorcism.

4

THIRTEEN YEARS OF CELIBACY

Although the exorcisms were noteworthy, my primary efforts in being heterosexual consisted of daily prayer, memorization of scripture, dating of women, confession of my temptations, total avoidance of pornography, and comprehensive reading of ex-gay literature. Some of the best-known authors were Frank Worthen, Leanne Payne, Joseph Nicolosi, Gordon Dalbey, Joe Dallas, Jeffrey Satinover, Mario Bergner, Bob Davies and Lori Rentzel, and Andrew Comiskey.

What these authors had in common was their belief that we are heterosexual by nature, and it is only because of damaged emotions and sinful choices that we engage in homosexual behavior and identify as gays or lesbians. The foundation of their beliefs was their Christian faith and their interpretation of the Bible.

I believed them, and they gave me comfort by explaining the reasons I struggled with homosexual feelings. I had been molested at a young age by an older male. My mother had been domineering and my father passive. My parents hadn't held, hugged, or cuddled me enough. I resented my mother and sisters, and this had created a fear and resentment of women.

I realize now how harmful these explanations are for gays and lesbians, but at that point in my life, I had no idea. No one concerns himself or herself with what causes heterosexuality. But gays and lesbians who cannot accept themselves, largely because of lack of communal acceptance, look to their childhoods for an explanation and for someone to blame, and these authors give them justification, and that is what happened with me. I blamed my uncle. I blamed my mother. I blamed my sisters, and I blamed my father.

Though my father was not physically affectionate, he was kind and loving, and he took good care of my mom and us children. He was a good listener, a thoughtful man, patient and reasonable, and he assumed the best about people. As a devout Roman Catholic, he shared the Christian faith of these anti-gay authors but had his own thoughts about homosexuality. He knew that I had struggled since childhood with anxiety and depression and how I had then struggled with my sexuality. He saw how I repeatedly began relationships with women, only to leave the women when they fell in love with me.

One day, he said to me privately, "Brian, I know it doesn't agree with the church, but it seems to me that some people are just born gay and should accept themselves the way they are."

It angered me that my own father would tempt me to be homosexual, and I told him so. "I feel like Satan is using you to tempt me, and I don't appreciate it. You know I don't believe that way, and I'm never going to believe that way."

He again acknowledged that it wasn't the teaching of the church, but he still believed that gay people existed and probably should accept themselves. Another time when he repeated these thoughts to me, I responded, "Some people are dead today because well-meaning people like you attempt to 'set us free,' and we get AIDS and die." As before, he readily acknowledged that his feelings differed from the church's teachings, but that's the way he believed.

In October 1996, I found a low-cost group counseling opportunity called the Living Waters program. It advertised itself as "an in-depth, Christ-centered healing discipleship program geared for men and women seeking sexual and relational wholeness in Christ." The group met on Tuesday nights from seven to ten o'clock for seven months. Each Tuesday, I drove forty-five miles to attend the meeting at the Anaheim Vineyard church in Southern California.

Although I found the Living Waters program insightful and encouraging, it was not a cure for me. I was relieved to meet other men and women like me who struggled with homosexual feelings, but I found myself longing for physical and sexual closeness with several other men in the program. Still, we signed a contract that we would not meet with each other outside of the program, not even in the parking lot to converse, and I complied with the agreement.

5

Time for a Therapist

For many years, I considered seeking individual therapy, but the costs seemed exorbitant. I repeatedly decided against spending the money, but circumstances eventually convinced me differently. On December 29, 1997, the day I returned to Southern California after my unfortunate argument with my mother over the open blinds, and after my conversations with my friends Dennis and Wade, I believed God said to me, "How would I convince you to spend the money? It's my money. If I want to give you three hundred dollars to replace it, I can. I could give you six hundred dollars if I want. It's my money. I want you to spend it on therapy."

I had been told by several counselors that three to five years or more of counseling might be needed, and yet that day I felt the liberty to spend up to three hundred dollars a month for as many years as necessary. I immediately began asking my colleagues at the missionary agency for referrals to a good therapist. They all recommended one particular man, Dr. William T. Ashman, a PhD clinical psychologist and executive director of Christ's Counseling Center, a Christian therapy team that specialized in sexual addictions as well as multiple personality disorder (MPD), now called dissociative identity disorder (DID); early childhood satanic ritual abuse; and spiritual warfare issues, including casting out demons. Dr. Ashman had a second office in a nearby city, and it was there where he worked with several families in our community.

Two days after I made the decision to seek a therapist, I left a message on his answering machine, explaining that I was a young man, age thirty-four, who struggled with homosexual temptations and wanted to be free from them. I particularly wanted to be healed from my longing for intimacy with men. My religious convictions would not allow me to experience this in a romantic or sexual relationship with a man. If I was to find this kind of intimacy, it would have to be either with a woman or in a nonsexual relationship with a man.

Dr. Ashman called me back and suggested I might work well with a close colleague named Timothy Neumann. Tim had interned at Christ's Counseling Center, and Dr. Ashman had invited him into a working partnership with four other therapists. Even more, it appeared he had taken on a fatherly and mentoring relationship with him.

On January 2, 1998, I called Timothy Neumann in San Fernando and left a lengthy message stating that Dr. Ashman was willing to work with me but wanted me to have the option of working with Tim, whom he described as a man who got up in the morning hoping to have the opportunity to encourage someone in this area of homosexuality. That same day, Tim called me back and described himself and Dr. Ashman as probably the most effective therapists in this area of expertise.

My first thought when I met Tim Neumann was how handsome he was and how kind. We made our way from the front waiting area to his office. It was tidy and clean and had a giant plant and family photos. I don't remember how we started our conversation, but I clearly remember that my primary goal was to find out whether he would he feel comfortable holding me as part of my therapy. I was convinced that my emotional healing was going to be the result of physical, but nonsexual, intimacy with a man. I wanted to be held more than anything in the world, and this, I believed, was the key.

I began to tell Tim my basic story, as to how I believed I had come to have homosexual feelings. I had been molested by my uncle when I was eight or nine; he was five and a half years older than I and had a post-pubescent body. I had grown up believing my mother and my two sisters hated boys, and I had intense feelings of resentment and anger toward them. I had been closest to my dad but never had been able to feel close to him physically and had been too afraid to ask him to hold me. Everything I told him was my way of laying a foundation to ask, "Will you hold me?" I wasn't likely to work with someone who wouldn't. Like a man dying of thirst who wanted only water, to be held was all I wanted.

After several minutes, and with careful consideration of each word, I asked, "Will you be willing to hold me if I feel like I need to be held?" Without hesitation, and as if speaking gently to a child, he said, "Yes, I will, but it is your job to ask. That's part of growing up—being able to ask for what you need."

I was elated but still had one more concern. I knew my desires to be held were intense. I could not feel safe if my therapist had sexual feelings for me. Somewhat sheepishly, I said, "I need to know that my therapist is not dealing with the same issues as I am. I cannot try to protect my therapist from myself."

He understood what I meant and said, "I've been happily married for twenty-five years, and I don't molest little boys." I broke into tears of relief and joy that I had found the perfect father figure to hold me and listen to me and assure me and give me all the love I thought I had missed out on from my own father.

I apologized for crying; I knew this was just supposed to be an interview. He said he knew I was the kind of person with whom he would love to work. Moving slightly forward, he looked me in the eyes and said, "You're really ready for this, aren't you?" Yes, I was, and yes, I believed God had brought us together. We discussed his fee, and when I told him I could spend $300 a month, he said that would be adequate, even if I came more than once a week, which he suggested initially. Sensing my anxiousness to get started, he offered to meet with me the next day. I assured him I could walk out that door, pull myself together, and become normal Brian again. He smiled and said he knew that, but if I felt the need, I could call, and he would meet with me the next day.

Somewhere in our conversation, the concept of spiritual adoption came up. This was an idea developed by Dr. Ashman and Tim. They believed that God called them occasionally to spiritually adopt a client. They treated the person as their own son or daughter. Both Dr. Ashman and Tim invited these clients to their homes to meet their wives, biological family, and other spiritual family for birthdays, holidays, and special occasions. A spiritual adoption was something believed to be initiated by God and had to be agreed on by both therapist and client. I immediately wanted to be adopted by Tim and hoped he wanted me in the same way.

6

Spiritual Grandpa

The following day, I met with Dr. Bill Ashman. I felt completely at ease. I told him how well things had gone with Tim. I was confident that unless Dr. Ashman specifically thought I should work with him, I wanted to work with Tim. He agreed and said Tim had already called and left a message on his machine saying, "I hope Brian picks me." Dr. Ashman assured me that when someone chose Tim, they got him as well since Dr. Ashman was supervisor.

"It's like getting two for the price of one," I said.

He smiled and agreed, explaining they would confer unless specifically asked not to. In our earlier conversation, Tim had referred to Dr. Ashman as his spiritual father, so I figured that if Tim adopted me, then Dr. Ashman would be my spiritual grandfather and I would have a therapist for a dad and a clinical psychologist for a granddad. What could be more perfect? While at Dr. Ashman's office, I picked up a copy of a booklet titled *Professional Therapy Never Includes Sex*, provided by the California Department of Consumer Affairs, the Board of Behavioral Sciences, in Sacramento.

I called Tim when I got back to my office and excitedly left him a voice-mail message. "It's a go. Just call and let me know what time."

Tim called back and indicated that we would meet in his San Fernando office the following Monday.

Dr. Ashman also provided me with a one-page explanation of spiritual adoption. Within it he had written, "Everyone enters God's family through spiritual adoption … This is not pretend … Spiritual families must provide more than hugs at church … We must also furnish birthday celebrations and Friday night suppers—like a family. This way we begin to see the faint outline of our real family … Adoptions are permanent. Each adoption requires the spiritual family to create a new spot. It will be uncomfortable but joyous! Move over and make some room."

I had expressed similar ideas over the years. Two years earlier, I had written in a missionary newsletter,

> We are brothers and sisters. We are fathers and mothers. Our homes are each other's. We are not pretending to be these things or pretending to have these relationships. We are truly related to one another by blood, Jesus's blood. "'Who is my mother and who are my brothers?' Jesus asked. He stretched out his hands toward his disciples and said, 'Here are my mother and my brothers! For whoever does the will of my Father in heaven is my brother and sister and mother.'" (Matthew 12:48–50)

In the same newsletter, I had written about touch:
> Do you ever think about how much time you spend each day in physical contact with another person? If you're single, you may find you have an average of about five to ten seconds of "touch time" per day. This might be made up of three two-second handshakes, two one-second pats on the back, and maybe a two-second hug on a good day. Children are the only people in our society who have the freedom to ask for and receive affection. People who are rarely or never touched dry up emotionally or compromise their morality to get the touch they want. I believe that most sexual immorality begins with a desire for intimacy. How many times have we heard the statement that girls are willing to be sexual in order to feel loved? What about boys? Do they do the same thing? Perhaps if dads and moms made sure to demonstrate their love for their children clearly, their children wouldn't be so quick to compromise their upbringing to feel another person's love.

7

In His Arms

On January 12, 1998, I met with Tim for our first official session. It was one of the most promising days of my life. When we began our session, he asked if I had any particular way I wanted to begin; I said I hoped he would lead. He asked me about my family. "How many brothers and sisters do you have? What kind of relationship do you have with your father? What kind of relationship do you have with your mother?" As I began telling my story, I started crying. He leaned forward and with gentleness asked, "What can I give you? What would you like from me?"

"I would like to be held, but I know I will just cry and cry, and I don't want to look like such a baby."

He asked, "Would it be okay to cry and cry and cry?"

Through my tears I explained that my mom had repeatedly called me a baby when I got upset as a child.

"I'm so sorry she said that to you," he said. He moved from his chair, sat beside me on the couch, held me, and let me cry. I did indeed cry for a very long time.

As the flood of emotion abated, I told Tim some of my earliest memories. I remembered sitting on the toilet at three or four years old and crying for my mommy to come and wipe me. I felt sad and alone. I cried out again and again for her to help me because I thought it would be gross to wipe myself.

I told him about my first day of kindergarten when I was too afraid to ask where the bathroom was and, when I couldn't hold it any longer, watched the urine run down my leg from my little pair of summer shorts, terribly ashamed and embarrassed in front of my teacher and fellow students. My father, who was the janitor at the school I attended, decided I should wear the same clothes the rest of the day. I suppose he thought it would teach me not to do it again.

I told Tim about my uncle starting me on sex when I was too young to understand what we were doing and about the guilt and fear and loneliness it had created. With each detail, the emotions were there as when I first experienced them.

"I'm sorry he did that to you," Tim said. "You are safe now. I won't let him hurt you again." Tim's body was warm. His heartbeat was steady. His arms were strong. I felt safe and cared for. I had been held many times during my three years of being gay at Chico State, but those embraces had not had the power of this experience.

We talked about spiritual adoption without specifically applying it to our relationship. It was too early to discuss this, and I was too raw emotionally to consider asking and possibly being rejected, a situation similar to that with my father, when I chose to not ask to be held rather than face the possibility of being told no.

When I climbed into my car to return home, I sobbed uncontrollably. I made sure the windows were secure and wailed like a woman mourning for a lost baby or young child. The depths of my years of longing overflowed the banks of my capacity to contain them. My years of loneliness, isolation, pain, grief, sadness, guilt, and fear were coming to an end. I was going to be okay. I was going to be held and nurtured and loved and cared for.

As I drove home, I made up "I love Dad" songs. I sang about loving my spiritual dad. Already, I felt like Tim's son, and I did not think that I might be investing too much emotionally in my therapist after this one session. In my journal notes, I wrote, "I wanted him so badly to be my dad. I thanked God for his marvelous ways, his answer to years of praying and seeking a father. I love him. He is my dad. We will always be father and son. Dr. Ashman is my granddad. He will always be my father also. I am loved. God adores me. He is in charge and taking perfect care of me. I think God is calling me into this kind of love relationships [spiritual adoption] for the rest of my life."

On the way home, I decided I would make a recording of my piano playing that night. I spent three hours at one of the pianos at the mission agency where I lived and recorded music with the theme of fatherhood. I titled the tape "Shepherd of My Soul," one of the song titles, and on the label, I wrote, "A Gift for Dad, From Brian" and "Performed on 1/12/98," as a reminder to both of us that this tape had been made the evening of the first day we officially met in session.

I was up until after midnight that Monday night. I listened to myself play. I held the recorder like a baby as I listened. I enjoyed my own playing and singing, and I knew Tim would as well. When I heard a mistake, it didn't bother me because I knew it would not bother Tim either. I felt like I was holding myself. I also already felt anxiety about losing him. I didn't know for sure yet what our relationship would become. I knew only that I desperately wanted a dad, and I hoped that he would be that dad. I wasn't sure how I could wait a whole week before seeing him again. I just wanted to be with him.

One of my editors commented here, "You were *in love* even if you didn't realize it that way at that point." I have contemplated his words again and again. I have not come to a conclusion.

Thinking back over this time period, I regret that I devalued my own father to the point of replacing him with Tim. How could I have been so needy, so empty, and so desperate that I would jump into the arms of a man I had met only a few days earlier?

8

Anxiety and Depression

Over the years, many of my behaviors and thinking patterns had been part of an attempt to calm myself down. When I was a boy, my mother had called me "worrier." Rather than assume that her label simply became a self-fulfilling prophecy, I suspect I really did exhibit the characteristic of worry from a young age, and she was simply identifying it and trying in her own way to shame me out of it, but unfortunately, it didn't work.

My Grandma Kraemer understood me. She was not only my grandmother but also a dear friend. She had suffered from a mental breakdown after her fifth of seven children and had to be hospitalized for a month. For nearly a year, she had been barely able to get out of bed. Finally one day, with sheer determination, she had forced herself to begin cooking, cleaning, and participating in the formerly normal routine.

She knew what it was to be a worrier, and worry she did until the last three years of her life, after nearly dying and then recovering. She enjoyed life much more after coming so close to death, I think because she no longer feared it. One time she shared with me that her father had spent two years in a mental hospital for depression.

As a young teenager, I found jogging daily helped significantly. Worry and the accompanying depression were mitigated by exercise. Whenever I was depressed, my dad asked, "Have you run today?"

During my relationship with Tim, I still suffered from severe anxiety and depression. I swam every other day and jogged three miles up a mountain on the other days. I also did many pushups, pull-ups, and sit-ups. Often I awoke between 2:30 and 5:30 a.m. and did forty-five minutes of sit-ups to work off my nervous energy. Only then was I tired enough to go back to sleep.

My mind was constantly active. I couldn't quiet my thoughts. On my hikes, I repeatedly told my brain, "Shhh. Be quiet." Other times, I was so angry and frustrated with my mental chatter, I yelled, "Shut up!" again and again, hoping for silence. I frequently enjoyed hiking my favorite trail, the Mt. Wilson Toll Road, in the nude. It seemed much more natural and relaxing to do so, and I avoided people for the most part.

Most afternoons, by 2:00 p.m., my shoulders were tight from tension, and I had trouble remembering people's names and phone numbers, things I normally remembered very easily. Sometimes my chest hurt, or I felt pressure in my ears.

I worked in a mission agency that required me to attend many meetings, and I hated sitting still that long. My legs ached. I massaged my arms or took off my shoes or stretched my legs in order to relax. After forty-five minutes, I was stressed out. Physical contact such as resting my hand on a friend's back helped me relax.

When I was in high school, I had panic attacks. My heart raced. I felt like I was going to die and needed to run away from wherever I was. I stopped having chronic panic attacks in my early twenties. I had one last attack around age thirty, and my response to the pounding heart and impending feelings of death was, "If I die, I die." I took a completely passive attitude of acceptance toward the fear, and I've never had another one since.

At the mission agency, my office was meticulously organized. My files had typewritten labels. I emptied trash cans before they needed to be. My mind was ever active. My mental experience was like having ten documents open on a computer desktop at a time and not being able to close them. I took my work home with me mentally. From the house, I listened to my work voice-mail messages and usually responded to them. Perhaps I needed other things besides work to occupy my time, but an unanswered voice mail felt like something out of place that needed to be put in order. I longed to obey the biblical commands to "be still and know that I am God," to "be anxious for nothing," and to "not worry about tomorrow" and to believe the promise that says, "Perfect love casts out all fear." It was with this level of chronic, daily anxiety and depression that I looked to Tim for help.

9

MAY I CALL YOU DAD?

The day after that first session, I started crying every time I thought about Tim. I wanted to be with him. I wanted him to hold me. I wanted to ask him, "May I call you Dad?" Even though Tim and I had talked about spiritual adoption, we had never said, "I want to be your dad" or "I want to be your son." I wanted to give him the tape I had prepared for him the night before, but I had written, "A Gift for Dad," and if he didn't want me to be his son, this might make him feel obligated to adopt me even if it wasn't his calling or inclination. I didn't want him to feel pushed in any way because then I could never feel confident in our relationship.

I began to think that even if he did say I could call him Dad, I would still wonder if he meant it. This thought of not knowing for sure was painful. After two hours of off-and-on crying, I decided that Tim would want for me to call. This new relationship had unleashed a flood of emotion that, for the most part, I had kept under control. Now, the hope of alleviating my pain was so great, I couldn't control my emotions. An infant may whimper from hunger, but he is still relatively quiet until a few inches from his mother's breast, at which point he begins to cry and grab in desperation.

I called Tim and left a message, telling him that I couldn't stop crying and wanted to ask him a question. I waited fifteen minutes but then left the office to talk to a staff member and friend at the agency where I worked. When I returned to my office, I typed out my feelings amid tears. The phone rang. It was Tim. Hearing his voice, I cried again on the phone. He said he was glad I had called.

I asked if I could read him what I had written. I didn't want to manipulate him or rush him into wanting to be my dad, I explained, but I wanted to ask, "May I call you Dad?" It occurred to me that perhaps my crying in itself was manipulative, and Tim might feel awkward saying no.

He said, "Brian, last night I was putting together a tape for you on spiritual adoption, and I wanted to include a letter with it and sign it, 'Love, Dad.' I was concerned that I might be rushing you, but it looks like you are ready. Yes, you may call me Dad." He asked if I would like to meet with him the next day, and I quickly said yes. I was elated but frightened. I wanted to try on the name "Dad," but not quite yet. It would sound fake, contrived, and unreal, not how I hoped to soon be able to say it with love and closeness.

10

SEXUALLY AROUSED

Wednesday morning, I arrived about twenty-five minutes early, and Tim arrived about five minutes late. I was anxious to give him my card and my tape. I gave them to him immediately along with a tape player, in case he didn't have one. He thanked me for them and said he really liked piano music. As we sat down, he asked whether I would like for him to sit next to me. I said yes immediately. I was feeling so many conflicting feelings. My need for physical touch was overwhelming.

He held me because I wanted to be held, but I felt sexually aroused. At first, I was afraid to tell him for fear he might stop holding me or be disgusted with me. Embarrassed, I told him about it. He said that this was normal because I had to learn how to be close without being sexual, that my body was responding automatically from the past, but over time the arousal would disappear. We talked about the difference between feeling *sexual*, which was genital, and *sensual*, which had to do with the senses, including touch. Learning how to be close without feeling aroused might take a year or two, but I shouldn't worry about it. He wasn't afraid of my arousal, so I didn't need to be. "After all," he said, "we get aroused for lots of different reasons, not just sexual ones."

I held him tighter. My feelings were so conflicted. One moment, I felt loved and accepted completely. The next moment, I felt scared, distant, intellectual, and cold. I wondered about the wisdom of this. I was emotionally throwing myself over a cliff and expecting Tim to catch me.

I thought about my homosexual relationships in college. My boyfriends and I would stare into each other's eyes and hold each other for hours. This felt the same. What if I was *in love* with Tim's body, but real love for him as a father never came? What if I turned cold on him and decided I didn't like him? What if we had nothing in common? I tried to say a little bit of this to him, but I couldn't explain myself. He said I was probably dissociating—a defense mechanism we use when we feel too much anxiety to stay in the moment. We distance ourselves from our feelings and instead experience a kind of "separateness" from ourselves. Daydreaming is a minor example of this, whereas dissociative identity disorder is an extreme example. Tim knew a lot about dissociation, more than I realized at this point in our relationship.

I looked into his eyes so that we could communicate face-to-face. I told him I felt like I wanted to crawl inside of him and stay there forever. He said we needed to slow down a little. I didn't know what he meant by that, but I trusted him. He looked me squarely in the eyes and smiled. "I really like you, son."

I responded, "I really like you too." I couldn't say the word. I began to talk about something else and then thought about why I couldn't call him Dad. "Tim, I want to change what I just said. When you said, 'I really like you, son,' I said, 'I really like you too,' but I didn't say what I want to say: I really like you too, Dad."

"Why couldn't you say it?" he asked.

I felt scared, like I was getting caught not really loving him like I should. To call him Dad felt awkward and contrived. I didn't want to get sucked into saying something I didn't mean. At the same time, I wanted to crawl inside this man and "stay there forever," as I had said. What was going on? In retrospect, was it possible that I was falling in love with Tim?

When I was ready to leave that morning, I needed to use the restroom, but the door was locked. I heard a toilet flush, and so I waited outside the door for someone to come out and let me in. Just then, Tim came into the hall to give me my tape recorder, which I had forgotten in his office. I asked whether he could let me into the restroom.

"Almost any key will do," he said. Because of a problem with the lock, almost any key would open it. I tried my house key. It opened.

A man exited at just that moment, and Tim and I both entered the restroom. He asked me, "How are you going to feel about standing next to Dad and peeing?"

"That'll be fine. I might have to multiply really large numbers."

"What?" he asked.

"I have a hard time starting to pee if there is someone standing next to me, but if I multiply large numbers, then I can relax enough to go."

He laughed.

After waiting for several seconds, I said quite boldly, "Four thousand, six hundred, and twenty-eight," as if I had been figuring out this huge number.

He laughed and said, "I can tell I'm really going to enjoy getting to know you."

Later that afternoon, I wrote in my journal, "I can stare into his eyes without him being afraid of the intimacy. I'm feeling sexually aroused just writing this. I'm not sure why. I only know that I really feel close to Tim, and yet I truly do not want to have sexual contact with him." Though I believed at the time I did not want to have sexual contact with him, it appears from my arousal that my body was thinking differently.

11

Many Intimate Friends

That afternoon, after returning from my counseling session with Tim, I handwrote an intimate, personal letter to one of my best friends at the mission agency where I lived and worked. He was my supervisor, and I was quite dependent on him as an older brother and father figure. I suspected he wasn't entirely comfortable with my neediness and repeated requests for assurance, and I was afraid he might pull away from me now that I had Tim. I wrote the letter because I wanted to affirm and secure his ongoing role in my life. I had hopes for more intimacy, not less.

January 14, 1998

Dear Todd,

You are incredibly special to me. You have taught me more about being loved and accepted than anyone in this community. I will never forget the day you said to me, "Brian, I want you to stop worrying about whether I love you or not. I do and I won't change my mind." I believed you that day and I still believe you. You set me free that day to believe that I am lovable and that I don't need to keep questioning you or making you prove it. I am very grateful for your heart toward me. The letter you wrote to me as a reference when I left to do support-raising read like a love letter, not like the boy-girl kind, but like the sincere heart of one friend to another. This is how I feel about you. Official or not official, you have acted as a brother to me and a father to me. I will always love you as both. This is not to put pressure on you, not at all. Love loves freely, not with expectations. My intention is to love freely. You have helped me to even learn how.

In a very real sense, I felt safe to love you because you first loved me. The relationship I am beginning to enjoy with Tim will never diminish my love for you. It will strengthen it and empower it. What began as dependency will mature into more love. I will always want to tell you things I don't tell others. I will want to trim hedges side by side with you. I will look on with admiration as you share yourself with [your wife] Sarah and with [your son] Bobby. I will consider you a father. I will want to rest my hand on my father's back. Please don't let me overwhelm you. I'm not asking or expecting you to do or be anything that you aren't already doing and being. Having a father's heart comes naturally to you. Respecting you and appreciating your heart comes naturally to me.

One last thing, love hurts. Sometimes it's very painful to love and sometimes it's very painful to be loved. I'm ready to take that chance. I expect nothing from you. I only hope that I might have an openness to receive any love you have for me and you might have an openness to receive any love I might have for you. Bless you, my dear friend.

Love,

Brian

In addition to Todd, I had many intimate friendships with men in our community. I could tell my friend Wade anything. He was a great listener and encourager. With a ready smile and a hand on my shoulder when I needed it, he always made me feel better. We routinely said "I love you" to each other without shame or embarrassment. I told him everything about my homosexual past, and though he didn't share the feelings, he listened without judgment. I had met Wade the first day I arrived at the agency. He worked in the graphics department, and when I entered his office, he swung around in his chair and greeted me with a big smile. I knew instantly we would be friends, and we still are to this day, though separated by a couple thousand miles.

Another friend named Kevin Mitchell was a big brother to me and, like Wade, had no judgments about my struggle with homosexual feelings. We also talked about everything and could say "I love you" to each other. He was married with four children, and I spent many hours several times a week in his home eating, playing games, washing dishes, and taking care of the kids. One of his brothers was gay and was HIV-positive, and Kevin maintained a loving relationship with him even though he considered homosexual behavior to be a sin.

Another family, the Poncers, with their six children, adopted me into their family. I spent even more time with them than with the Mitchells. I loved babysitting the children while Alex and Abigail had a date night. I cleaned house, washed dishes, folded clothes, rocked the baby, and serenaded the kids on the piano.

If I had accepted myself as gay during this time, I could have fallen in love with any of these men: Todd, Wade, Kevin, or Alex. They all were exceptionally attractive men, physically and emotionally. I always surrounded myself with attractive men and still do.

Every morning from 8:00 to 8:45, the staff members of our missionary agency held a meeting. I always made a point of sitting between two male friends and putting my hands on their backs. I soaked in their masculinity, their boyishness, their power and strength and love. In spite of receiving their permission, I agonized daily over whether they were comfortable with my touch. Despite being a bit perturbed by my need to keep checking, they never rejected me. I was mostly afraid they might think my touch was sexual, which I was confident it wasn't. I never felt sexually aroused by this contact like I felt with Tim.

It is only as I look back on this seemingly insatiable need for touch and affection and assurance that I realize my behavior was largely the result of a chemical imbalance in the brain called obsessive-compulsive disorder (OCD). The fear and isolation I had felt after being molested by my uncle became my obsession, and the accompanying compulsion was to seek consolation in the arms of a father figure, a compulsion that remained with me and led me to the counseling office and arms of Timothy Neumann.

12

It's Working!

Within the first week, Tim told me about the upcoming birthdays of his son and wife. I wanted to meet the rest of his family, but I wasn't sure what to expect as Tim's latest son. I chose my words carefully, and referring to myself as if I were a newborn, I said I would like to attend if I was "old enough to bring home from the hospital." Afraid this might be too forward, I quickly acknowledged that I was "just barely born into the family and maybe not ready to come home." He said I would soon be able to meet his wife, Linda, and his son, Stuart, but he was busy for the next couple of weekends. I understood, although I was anxious to spend as much time with him and his family as possible.

I soon found out just how large this family was. Tim and Linda had two biological children: their son Stuart, who was seven, and their daughter Carla, who was nineteen and away at college. Tim also had three spiritually adopted children: Susan, an adult female client suffering from dissociative identity disorder; Tami, an adult female client; and Brent, an adult male client who had disappeared and didn't want contact with Tim anymore. I was now the fourth spiritual adoptee, and within a few months, there would be a fifth.

I knew spiritual adoption was unique. I had never heard of another therapist who adopted his clients, with the exception of Dr. Ashman, and to date I still have never heard of such a thing. I'm confident that Dr. Joseph Nicolosi, author of *Reparative Therapy of Male Homosexuality*, would reject the idea that spiritual adoption has anything to do with reparative therapy, but I would argue that these two men took the therapy to its logical fulfillment.

Although it was a clear violation of traditional therapeutic ethics, and not part of any program of reparative therapy of which I was or am aware, I considered Dr. Ashman and Tim innovative and courageous men.

Within a few days of our first counseling session, I already noticed changes in my thinking habits that suggested I was being healed from my homosexual temptations. While swimming at a local university pool, I noticed how little interest I had in looking at other men's bodies while they were swimming. In fact, most of my swimming time was spent counting laps and praying for Tim. In the shower, I was not nearly as self-conscious about my body as I usually was or concerned about getting aroused. I constantly thought about Tim, so much so, in fact, that I felt scared about being so attached to this man so quickly, but then I reassured myself that God had chosen us for each other.

I also noticed that I was not masturbating as much. Though I was still rubbing myself a bit, I didn't feel compelled to bring myself to orgasm but instead felt relaxed and able to quickly fall asleep. By simply thinking about Tim, I felt calm. In our time together, we had discussed masturbation briefly. When I told him I often masturbated, he replied, "I'd be concerned if you didn't." We laughed, and surprisingly, his acceptance of me didn't increase the desire, but seemed to lessen it.

I wondered what it would be like to see him again the following Monday. I seemed to be idealizing our relationship, even romanticizing it, making it unrealistic. I thought that Tim could do no wrong and that he loved me without reservation or hesitation. I thought we were really family, not just like family. I wondered what the relationship might cost me in the long run. I wasn't sure I wanted the responsibility of being that close.

I also thought about how human Tim was. He had already told me he took Zoloft, for depression, I believed. He described himself as a different man when he was on it. I wanted to love him in his weakness, maybe even because of his weakness. My feelings for him reminded me of my feelings for Todd, who also suffered from depression.

13

Early Sessions

As I look back on my counseling sessions with Tim, I'm embarrassed by the childishness of my behavior. It is difficult for me to understand how I could have been so convinced that these experiences were my route to emotional healing and freedom from unwanted homosexual temptations. My chief desire as I drove to Tim's office every Monday and Wednesday was to be held. Being held felt like the answer to my longing since childhood.

I would not have felt comfortable with this level of intimacy with Tim if not for the fact that he thought of me as—and I thought of myself as—a small child. We believed I was emotionally damaged, and the road to healing would be Tim's unconditional love and support and my trust in him. He would fill my emotional deficits by being a physically present father figure. His love would "stick" and be internalized, and I would no longer feel needy and empty, but would feel whole and complete. Dr. Nicolosi (1991), writing about a traditional therapeutic relationship says, "The client sees the therapist through the eyes of the child he once was. Transferred feelings include fear, anger, aggressive-defensive reactions, and sexual desires" (p. 169).

I clung to Tim like an infant many times, particularly in the first sessions when I discussed my earliest memories. We sat on the couch together, and I leaned my head against his chest with my arms around him. I liked to listen to his heartbeat and repeatedly told him so. After a while, I switched my position so that I could lean my back against him and tell him my thoughts more comfortably. I thought about what a child might want from his father and then proceeded to try it or ask for it. For example, I gently pulled the hairs on his arms although I feared he might stop me. Later, I massaged his forearms and hands and he did not pull away.

Over the first few months of sessions, the level of physical intimacy increased to the point where I took my shirt off several times so that I could lean against Tim with my bare skin. At my suggestion, he unbuttoned his shirt or let me do it so that I could put my arms around him and lean my chest against his. At least once, he took his shirt off completely. He locked the door when we did this, which felt scary because it reminded me of when I was a child and my uncle and I hid our sexual behavior behind locked doors.

One may wonder what I could have talked about for months of sessions. This was not the first time I was recounting the details of my life. I had told many people throughout the years, seeking catharsis and absolution in the telling. The key themes were being molested, becoming sexually involved with neighbor boys, feeling guilty and afraid, feeling isolated from my parents, developing fearful obsessive-compulsive symptoms, arguing with and resenting my mom and my sisters, having panic attacks in high school, confessing everything to my father at age ten, and then confessing everything again to my high school counselor in my sophomore year following a panic attack and continuing to meet with him until graduation.

Tim and I thought he could play the role of nurturing father, physically available and unconditionally loving and accepting. Over months and perhaps even several years, I would identify with his masculinity and "grow up" to be like him, a heterosexual male. Our thinking about "healing homosexuality" came largely from the writings of Dr. Joseph Nicolosi.

14

Accused

Thursday, January 29, 1998, began like any other day at the mission agency. Our morning meeting ended between 8:45 and 9:00 a.m. as it always did. On my calendar, a note read simply, "After morning meeting, meet with Leonard." Leonard Billings, the executive director of our mission agency, had asked me to see him in his office immediately after our group meeting. This day, although it had begun as any normal day, would be the beginning of the most frightening experience of my adult life. I had worked at the agency for three and a half years, had grown quite at home, was well respected, and had been given responsible positions, including being an assistant to the founder, Dr. Rudolph Clemens.

When I entered Leonard's office, he looked upset. He said, "Brian, James Evans has accused you of sexually molesting him. His father Harold is going to be calling on the phone from Australia in a couple minutes to confront you." James Evans was a grandson of the founder of the agency. His mother, Tonya, was a daughter of the founders, Dr. Rudolph and Mrs. Estel Clemens.

I had begun working there on September 6, 1994, and this family then moved into the community in 1995 and lived there until moving to Australia in 1997. James suffered from some kind of mild autism and spoke with a pronounced stutter. He was intelligent but had difficulty communicating with people because of the intensity with which he spoke and the way he got hung up on issues and expressed himself about them.

His grandmother, cofounder of the agency, told me at the time that James had been molested when he and his parents were missionaries in Algeria, and now he suffered from severe emotional problems and at times was suicidal. His grandmother was concerned that because he had been molested by a male, he might struggle with homosexual feelings. She and I talked about my early sexual experiences and my struggle with this, and I said I would be willing to meet with him and encourage him to talk if this was part of his problems.

Though I had intended many times to meet with him, it never worked out. Instead, my only interactions with James had been fairly negative. One day he asked me my name, and I responded, "Mr. Kraemer." Not satisfied, he asked me again. Being a school teacher and a substitute teacher at this mission agency's elementary school, I repeated that my name was Mr. Kraemer. I considered it disrespectful for a child to call an adult by his first name. He would not let the issue drop, nor would I give in. Later, his mother came to me and pleaded with me to compromise on this because of his condition, but I insisted that it was not a necessary compromise and that any child could learn how to call someone Mr. Kraemer. I considered him rebellious. Later, the family moved to Australia, and until this meeting with Leonard, I hadn't heard of them since their move.

Now, without warning, I was being told that this boy had accused me, along with one of my housemates, a man from Algeria, of molesting him. Later, I found out he had begun making these accusations more than a year earlier to his therapist in Southern California, Dr. Bill Ashman, the same clinical psychologist I considered my spiritual granddad. After listening to the then-sixteen-year-old James Evans's accusations, and even making recordings of them, Dr. Ashman had informed the leadership of the mission agency in early 1997, unbeknownst to me.

Now, a year later, James Evans's father, Harold, was about to confront me through a phone call from Australia. As our executive director told me this, he said, "I want you to know I would trust you with my own children." With tears, he added, "I'm very sorry this is happening."

My legs became weak. I felt faint. I thought, *My God, what's happening?* I sat down. "How can this be?" I said, confused and afraid.

Leonard repeated, "James has been saying that you molested him."

"But I didn't!" I protested.

"I'm so sorry this is happening," Leonard repeated.

Within a short time, the phone rang, and Leonard answered it using the speaker phone. Harold was angry and accusing, and it was obvious he believed his son. I told him it wasn't true, but he insisted he believed his son. I felt helpless and angry and confused and frightened. I knew protesting, arguing, or repeating my innocence was not going to help. Harold said I needed to stop my involvement in anything that had to do with children.

I was very active in caring for children in two families in the community, the Poncers and the Mitchells. I also was supposed to start tutoring two boys in math that morning at 9:30, and it was nearing that time. "But I'm tutoring two boys in math," I said.

Harold angrily replied, "No, you're not. You are not allowed to be alone with children at all."

I looked to Leonard and said, "Leonard, can I at least meet with them in a public place, where there will be other people around?"

Harold's voice boomed over the speaker phone, "No! You are not allowed to be with any children!"

I felt so angry. Harold was the son-in-law of the founder of this agency. He was also the man who held my future in his hands at that moment. He was taking control over my life. He thought me a child molester and wasn't hesitant to say so.

I don't remember the rest of the conversation. I think some discussion transpired of how to proceed. Harold said they could turn this case over to the local police and have them investigate me, but our organization's leaders preferred to put together a four-member panel of people within our agency to do the investigation while seeking advice from legal professionals. This was not a routine way of handling an accusation of molestation, but James's parents and grandparents knew he suffered from severe emotional problems and could possibly be making this up. They also knew I had an excellent reputation, was an elementary school teacher, and was trusted by the families in our community. Harold, his wife Tonya, and I agreed to the creation of the panel.

I was assumed to be a child molester by James's parents, and I had no idea who else they might have talked to. Tonya had three sisters, and I thought it likely she had talked to them already. I had to prove my innocence, but how in the world could I do that, and why would James say this about me?

As I returned to my office, I was dazed, confused, angry, and terribly frightened. My whole professional life was threatened. And with whom could I possibly speak about this? James was probably seventeen now. I wasn't sure.

People don't believe children lie about such things. One is assumed guilty until proven innocent when a child makes a sexual accusation against an adult. I again wondered who might know about this and how they might be looking at me. I had loved children so much up to that point. I always had known that I would make a wonderful dad. I loved to hold babies, rock them to sleep, play with them, and read to them. Now, I imagined I was presumed to be a child molester, and every glance toward a toddler or a baby could be interpreted as a sexual leer. "Oh, God, help me," I cried.

15

Could I Have Done It?

I contacted Tim immediately and told him how confused and frightened I was. He assured me that everything was going to be okay and reminded me that we would be able to see each other the following Monday. Handing over a check for $300 that morning a few days later seemed like nothing given the desperation I was feeling and the comfort I received from our relationship. I told him everything about the situation and discovered he already knew about it. He and Dr. Ashman had already discussed the accusations made by James Evans against me. James had been in therapy for more than a year with Dr. Ashman.

That morning, I told Tim everything I could think of that might have caused James to dislike me or target me for an accusation. Everything going on in my life was secondary now to this overwhelming and frightening situation. Tim listened intently to everything I said but then made a subtle comment that suggested I possibly could have molested this boy.

Incredulous and angry, I said, "What do you mean? How could you think I would do this?"

Quietly, he said, "Well, it's possible you could have done it and could not know you did it." He paused for a moment. "You could have multiple personalities and not know it."

I felt dizzy. "Multiple personalities?" A wave of fear coursed through my body. "I could have multiple personalities and not know it, and one of those personalities could have molested James?" My heart pounded in my chest. My mind raced. I felt panicky, nauseous, and confused.

Seeing my fear, Tim held me tighter. I pulled away in anger. I protested, but my thoughts were racing, imagining what evils I could be guilty of without knowing. Tim tried to assure me that everything was going to be okay, even if I had multiple personalities. He and Dr. Ashman and their colleagues were experts in these things. I was in the best place for getting help if this was part of my emotional problems. Perhaps this was why God had brought me to Tim and his team of experts in the first place.

Tim's suggestion to me that I might have multiple personalities and be guilty of committing this crime against James was one of the worst of his violations against me. Without symptoms of this severe mental disorder, it was terribly unprofessional, bordering on cruel, to make this suggestion to me, especially given my history of symptoms of OCD.

That day, as I drove home from his office, I thought about the possibility that I might not be in control of my own mind and behavior, that I could possibly have multiple personalities, each one unaware of the others and each one engaging in behaviors I couldn't allow to come to my memory. How could I know for sure whether I was crazy? What signs should I be looking for? I searched my mind for any thoughts or pictures of James naked. I searched every memory and thought that could include the slightest suggestion of my having molested this boy, but I couldn't think of anything. I looked at my odometer and thought, "I need to make sure I can account for every mile I put on my car. If I notice there are miles I can't account for, I might be going places and doing things with another personality." The thought terrified me.

When on campus at the agency, I concentrated on my every move and action, trying to make sure that I did everything with full awareness and that there were no blackouts or periods of empty, unaccounted-for time. What had been a bad dream up to this point had become a nightmare.

16

Letters to My Parents

It was time to tell my parents about this new therapeutic relationship with Tim. I chose not to mention anything to them about the accusation of molestation. Later, I did tell my father, but I thought it would be an unnecessary burden to my mother. In the first week of February, I wrote two lengthy letters describing in great detail my relationship with Tim. This was the first time I had ever communicated to my parents how strong my desire was to be physically intimate with a man while not being expressly sexual. I wrote, "I'm frustrated that after thirteen years of rejecting overt homosexual behavior, I feel internally as homosexually-oriented as I ever was. That's the sad reality of my feelings." I also asked an important question: "Is there some way I can satisfy my desire for male love without satisfying my desire for male sex? I would like to think my deepest longing for men is not for sex, but for love, but I'm not honestly sure."

My parents' response to this letter was silence because they didn't want to say anything to upset me. They knew I probably wouldn't listen anyway because I already knew what I needed. My mom later told me that she had thought, *Brian's gone off the deep end if he needs that much attention. This is what happens when you have children one right after the other. Brian is still trying to get the attention he didn't get when he was a child.* In 1966, my mom had three babies in diapers and raised us at a time when husbands provided minimal care for the children. Thinking about that time period, she still cries when she considers how overwhelmed she was, wanting to give us the attention we deserved, but not being able to do so.

Though perhaps she wasn't as available as she wanted to be when I was a child, at this point in my life, she and my dad were readily available, something I specifically noticed in contrast to Tim. Because I could not see him whenever I wanted, I wrote him lengthy letters expressing my feelings. I wrote how much I missed him and how afraid I was of losing him. I was also angry because there were so many differences between how he treated his biological children and how he treated me. I asked him whether he was as much my dad on weekends as on Mondays and Wednesdays. I wanted to know whether I could call him anytime just to talk without having a reason.

I also feared he would reject me and encouraged him to do so as soon as possible so it wouldn't hurt so much later. I wrote, "Your love can't be true. You can't stand up under the responsibility of a very, very needy son who is thirty-four years old. I want you to reject me now. Please don't let me fall in love with you only to find out I can't really be your son, not just like a son or a son sometimes or a convenient son. I want to be your real son." This plea is further evidence that I might have been falling in love with Tim without acknowledging it.

17

Penis Size and Underwear Brand

The four-member panel that was established to investigate the accusations made against me by James Evans was composed of Kim Adams, our director of administration and finance; Dr. Jonathan P. Ingham, a pastoral counselor and executive director of Counseling Center for Spiritual Warfare; Leonard Billings, the executive director of our mission agency; and Dr. Bill Ashman, the same clinical psychologist I then considered my spiritual granddad. Kim was responsible for overseeing the work of the panel, whose chief purpose was to vindicate me and prove my innocence. If at any time during its investigation the panel came to believe the allegations were true, the case would be turned over to local police.

Kim was a thoughtful, intelligent, and professional woman. She had moved to the United States as a child from Southeast Asia. Standing a little over five feet tall, she carried herself with authority, confidence, and kindness and commanded respect. She asked me to prepare a detailed written list of everything I did in a typical week. She also made an appointment for me to meet with Leonard and Dr. Ingham for an interview.

When I arrived for the interview, I had no idea what I might be asked. I knew our executive director well but knew Dr. Ingham only indirectly. He had a great reputation in our community for being a sensitive counselor and an expert in spiritual warfare, which included casting out demons. He was supervisor to Larry Myer-Stevens, the counselor with whom I had met for several months a year earlier and who had attempted to cast out demons of homosexuality.

Because James Evans had accused me of molesting him, they asked me to describe my body in detail, particularly my genitals. They seemed embarrassed, but I wasn't, so we had a good laugh over the situation. Did I have warts, moles, tattoos, birthmarks, scars, or anything else unusual about my body? Was I circumcised or uncircumcised? What did my penis look like when flaccid? What were my penis length, girth, and angle of erection when erect? What kind of underwear did I wear? What did I, or didn't I, wear to bed? I was asked to share anything at all that James should know if I molested him. His therapist in Australia would ask him to provide details about these things in order to establish my innocence.

They told me that James claimed I molested not only him, but also several other children in our community. He said I gave them drugs and threatened to hurt them or their families if they told. He said the abuse happened many times in many different places with many children and many perpetrators, including one of my housemates, Ahmed. I was assured that these allegations were being shared with only the minimum number of community members needed in order to prove my innocence. The panel would need to interview the families with whom I spent the most time. The parents would be asked to interview their children in such a way as to identify any possible abuse without suggesting it. I was sad at the thought of my closest friends being told about this and having to interview their children.

After the interview, Leonard walked with me to the rented four-bedroom home I shared with Ahmed and five other men who worked for the agency. There, he took photographs of my bedroom, our bunk beds, and underwear from my dresser. James claimed that most of the molestations had taken place in my bedroom. I doubted that he had ever been in our home, so these photographs and the information I provided in the interviews would be crucial to proving his accusations false. I hoped and prayed that the therapist in Australia would be wise enough to interview him carefully and not disclose to him any of the information we provided her about my body and my home.

By February 25, Tim and I had begun to routinely e-mail each other. Tim had a chat room established once a week for men struggling with homosexual feelings. I tried to make the time to participate from my work computer at the mission agency, but participation in the chat room was scarce, and it quickly became boring.

18

GOING HOME FOR THE FIRST TIME

On Sunday, March 1, 1998, I wrote the check for $300 and made it out to "Dad Neumann" and wrote in the memo line, "For our expenses." This felt a lot more satisfying than simply writing a check to Timothy Neumann. After all, who paid his dad for therapy? This felt a lot more like family. I didn't want to pay a therapist for counseling. I wanted to contribute to our family's needs.

On Monday morning, I gave Tim the check and explained why I had made it out the way I did. He smiled and said he enjoyed the sentiment. "Thanks, son." Our session continued, and this turned out to be the day, two months into therapy, that I was finally invited home! I was going to meet his wife, Linda, and their son, Stuart, and even stay overnight with them. Tim explained that every adoption was individual, and it was up to his wife to decide whether she would adopt me. I hoped she would so that our family would be complete.

On Wednesday afternoon, I drove the fifty miles to his home. I was thrilled to be meeting my possible spiritual mom and brother. When I arrived, only Tim was home, and though he was happy to see me, he also was distracted. We spent the afternoon doing errands. We picked up Stuart from school and shopped for dinner. Linda wasn't going to be home until late, so we ate and put Stuart to bed.

What I mostly wanted was to cuddle with Tim. Once Stuart was asleep, we sat together on the couch and held each other like we did in the office. We caressed each other's shoulders and arms. I played with the hair on his arms as I usually did. He always started to fall asleep whenever we held each other like this. He said Linda would be home soon.

I knew that when she arrived, he was going to jump up and move away from me before she came into the house. Sensing this, I told him it bothered me that once the garage door started to go up, I was going to have to scoot over, and we were going to have to stop holding. "It feels like we're doing something we shouldn't be rather than something very good and normal," I said. I wanted to be as open with Linda as I was with Tim. *Certainly, she must understand these things if he has other adopted children*, I thought.

Tim then told me about another member of this family, his spiritual brother Paul Martin. He explained that he and Paul enjoyed a lot of physical closeness as well, and though Linda knew Tim found their physical contact healing, she didn't want to know about it. The implication was she wouldn't want to know about Tim's and my physical affection either.

The garage door began to rise, and Tim rose with it. I didn't let this bother me and reminded myself that this was my first meeting with Linda, and certainly it would be better if she didn't make my acquaintance by seeing me cuddling with her husband on their couch. I was already planning, however, to ask her permission once we knew each other better. I was sure *Mom* wouldn't mind my closeness with *Dad*, and this openness would make our closeness even more wonderful. Perhaps I could even have this closeness with her.

I hoped I might be able to feel close to Linda. I had never felt physically intimate with a woman, not even on a platonic level. Though I knew my mother loved me and had held me as an infant, I had no memories of being cuddled, stroked, or consoled. I had held girlfriends and been held by girlfriends, but my constant thought was how I would prefer to be with a man.

When Linda got home, she looked tired. Although polite, she said little and went to bed after only twenty minutes. I didn't mind because I wanted more time with Tim. Once Linda was in bed, Tim suggested we go to the room where I was going to sleep and wrap a birthday present for Andy, his most recent spiritually adopted son. Andy lived in Pennsylvania and suffered from severe multiple personality disorder and was suicidal.

It was already 8:30 p.m., my usual bedtime, and I still had had hardly any time being held by Tim. I said, "Dad, do you mind if I climb into bed, and you just lie beside me and hold me?"

He said, "No, that's fine." I was beginning to take off my pants to climb into bed when he asked, "Do you mind my being here when you take your pants off?"

"No, it's no problem," I said. I crawled into bed, and Tim lay down beside me and held me. I was still wearing the T-shirt I had worn all day and my underwear. Tim was on top of the blankets. I was inside of them.

After a while, I felt too hot to wear my T-shirt. I asked, "Dad, do you mind if I take my shirt off? I'm too hot."

"No, that's fine," he said.

I took off my shirt. We continued to hold. I felt sexually aroused by our contact and told him. He asked whether I wanted him to stop holding me. "No, I want to get past the arousal," I said. I thought it would be only a matter of time before I stopped feeling aroused and just felt loved and secure in our father–son relationship.

After a few more minutes, Tim asked, "Do you want Dad to take his shirt off too?"

"Sure. That would be nice."

We continued holding and massaging each other. It felt incredibly intimate, but also confusing. My intimacy with Tim felt like that of my three sexual relationships with men in college. Everything felt the same except that there was no directly sexual contact as we were defining it. Tim and I had discussed in his office the difference between sexual and sensual. Sexual was genital–genital, mouth–mouth, or mouth–genital contact. It appeared to me that most anything else was simply sensual and was okay.

I stroked Tim's back, stomach, ears, moustache, nose, face, and underarms, all over above his waist. I loved having the freedom to explore him. I also was intensely sexually aroused. My penis was very uncomfortable in my underwear, and I told Tim. He said I could "rearrange" myself if I wanted, or I could take them off. I chose to move my penis into a position where it could be erect while I still wore my underwear. This was not visible to Tim because I was under the blankets. After a short while, still uncomfortable, I took them off and told Tim. I stayed under the blankets.

We continued to hold, stroke, and caress, exploring one another. I felt happy to have no fear, embarrassment, or rejection, just absolute acceptance and affirmation. I felt free to fart when I needed to, to say what touch felt good, to explore Tim's body. I thought, *I can even be erect, the worst thing possible in terms of embarrassment for me, and not be judged or rejected. I am safe. This is terrific.* I also felt confused by how sexual this felt to me and how Linda, in a nearby room, would feel about this. I asked myself, *Am I committing adultery?* I put those thoughts out of my mind and continued to enjoy Tim. He suggested we might soon be able to spend a whole night together at a cabin I knew about. Then he could hold me all night. It seems to me now that perhaps Tim was falling in love with me as well.

19

I Feel Sick Inside

On Friday, I wrote a letter to Dr. Ashman and explained everything that had happened Wednesday night. I began the letter, "I'm feeling kind of sick inside. What I mean is that I am concerned about my relationship with Dad Neumann." Later I said, "I am still feeling a 'sick feeling' and kind of want to cry. I really, really don't want to lose Dad and I really, really don't want to not be able to be close to him. I long for intimacy with him, not sexual contact, but the kind of which I am about to tell you happened on Wednesday night."

I could not remember a time when being touched wasn't sexual. Although certainly my parents had held me as an infant, I wasn't able to recall a single experience of being held or cuddled by either of them. The only holding I remembered was from my uncle, and it was expressly sexual. I wanted so much for my physical intimacy with Tim to be okay, to be a good thing, a wholesome closeness, even a transformative experience that bonded father and son and that would permanently heal my emotional feelings of loneliness.

I finished my letter to Dr. Ashman by saying,

> I love this man. He has been so good to me. I want to stay with him. If we can be this intimate and still be in God's will, I want more. I'm ready to dive in head first and bask, soak in closeness. I've wanted this kind of intimacy as long as I can remember. More than this, though, I want God's will. I want intimacy with God and I want to do those things that God leads me into to mature as

a man, to grow safely as a boy and then to move on into manhood. I'm not afraid of unusual or innovative ways of being healed. I'm willing to be odd, but I'm crying out to you to help us know if what we are doing and experiencing is okay. Is this healing for me or is this a clever, disguised form of homosexual behavior, simply redefining words like sexual and sensual and closeness and love? I'm afraid of losing Dad. I'm afraid of not being able to be close to him like I want. I'm afraid that maybe we're fooling ourselves. Please help me understand what we're doing. I have told Dad I feel safer with him because he is your son. My safety with Dad depends a lot on my trust in you as his father. I have referred to you often as grandpa to him. I sincerely appreciate your kindness, wisdom, and insight. I am seeing Dad again on Monday.

I e-mailed Tim a copy of everything I sent to Dr. Ashman. Over the weekend, Dr. Ashman called and said he wanted to meet with Tim and me Monday morning. He sounded concerned and serious. Tim also contacted me and assured me that everything was going to be okay. He let me know he and his family were moving in two weeks to live with his spiritual brother, Paul, and Paul's two young boys, about Stuart's age. He also said he liked the idea of us going to the cabin together soon.

Monday morning, I met with Tim and Dr. Ashman, who was still very sober. Dr. Ashman said we were both moving along way too fast and needed to slow down. Specifically, he said that whenever I became sexually aroused, therapy had stopped. I was relieved to have revealed our behavior to the man I called Granddad and not have him get angry or end our relationship or tell us we couldn't be close anymore, all which I feared might happen. I felt safe that he knew, and I also felt safe because I knew I could always bring anything to his attention, and Tim had been put on notice that he better behave responsibly as a father and a therapist. I had proven I wasn't going to keep secrets, and the safety of having both a dad and a granddad was comforting. With this revelation, Tim and I could continue to build our father–son relationship with care. Ultimately, it was Tim's responsibility to know what was right or wrong, safe or unsafe, and I felt a renewed assurance that he knew what he was doing.

On Wednesday, we had our usual appointment, and Tim was more cautious than previously. He put more effort into staying aware of how I was doing and whether I felt safe. I felt a certain hesitation in him that I didn't like. My mind was trying to figure out how I could most quickly get us back to where we had been, feeling safe cuddling and holding each other. What I wanted was the touch and the feeling that I could do whatever I wanted, like a young son. I knew that children did whatever they felt like doing with their parents, and it was entirely the parents' responsibility to set limits. I tried putting my hand inside Tim's shirt as I had done previously, and he gently moved my hand away. He would no longer let me unbutton his shirt as he had in the past. He was setting limits. This made me feel both safe and frustrated.

I still considered his holding and touch therapy. My path to heterosexuality required that I fully identify with my father, with his masculinity, and with his love for women. I had doubts about what Tim and I were doing, but I believed that Tim was heterosexual and that he knew the path I needed to travel in order to become heterosexual as well.

20

Hooked Up to a Polygraph Machine

In March, the four-member panel sent me to a professional polygraph examiner in Los Angeles named Joseph Paolella. He was considered the best in the business. I was frightened about going to a polygraph expert because I was sure that my body was going to say I was guilty even if my mouth said I was innocent. Furthermore, I didn't even know whether I was innocent because Tim had told me I could be dissociative, have multiple personalities, and not even know what I had done. My reputation and future lay in the results of this test. I was terrified. I drove into Los Angeles with the directions I had written out and made my way to the office of Dr. Chris Gugas & Associates on Wilshire Boulevard.

When I entered the room, I was surprised by how simple and undecorated the office was. It obviously was a working office, but there was no evidence of anything modern or contemporary in its décor. There were a few chairs where I could sit down. On the wall above the chairs were photographs of the examiner, Joseph Paolella, with former president John F. Kennedy. This man was obviously a professional even if his office didn't announce it. Mr. Paolella had been a special agent with the US Secret Service and had worked with the White House Protective Service Detail under four presidents.

I sat and waited nervously for Mr. Paolella, who finally came out and invited me to follow him down the hallway into his office on the right. There were papers, folders, books, and files everywhere. He motioned for me to sit down and asked me to explain why I was there. I told him that I had been falsely accused by a boy of molesting him and that the four-member panel of our mission agency had asked whether I would be willing to take a polygraph test. He asked whether I knew anything about how a polygraph test was done. I told him I was very frightened by the whole process because I was sure that my fear about the results of the test would make it look like I was guilty even though I wasn't. To complicate things even more, my therapist had told me I could be dissociative and have multiple personalities and not even know whether I did this or not, I explained. Seemingly unaffected, Mr. Paolella told me that the panel had sent him a list of nearly a hundred questions and that polygraph tests were not done that way. At the most, he could ask me maybe five questions, but probably even fewer than that, basically whether or not I molested James Evans. He was a very no-nonsense kind of guy, pleasant and kind, but not particularly demonstrative and definitely unpretentious and practical.

Besides providing testing, Mr. Paolella also trained students out of his office. He asked whether I would meet with a small class of trainees before being hooked up to the polygraph machine. I agreed, thinking it would be advantageous to have more people involved in discerning my honesty. Mr. Paolella sent me to the end of the hall, where the students appeared to be waiting for me. They asked me first why I was there. I explained as carefully as I could. They then asked for more details. We spent perhaps ten or fifteen minutes together and the time seemed surprisingly lighthearted and comfortable, even at times eliciting a few laughs.

Mr. Paolella returned to the room and asked me to follow him to another room where the polygraph machine was located. We were now alone and remained alone for the rest of our time together. I sat in the chair set up for me, and he hooked me up to the multiple attachments, including two on my fingers, a blood pressure gauge on my left arm, and two elastic bands around my abdomen and chest measuring upper and lower respiratory movements. I felt like a criminal. How could I, Brian Kraemer, have gotten into this position where I was now fitted like a perpetrator, a child molester, an evil person, and I couldn't even be sure I didn't commit the crimes? Did I really believe I could have multiple personalities? Absolutely, and it frightened me terribly.

He told me he needed to establish some baseline measurements, so he would ask me to simply say yes or no to very simple questions. He showed me a nickel and asked, "Is this a nickel?"

I replied, "Yes."

"Is Brian Kraemer your name?"

"Yes."

"Is this a nickel?"

"No."

He asked me several questions and then told me he was going to ask the question about James Evans. I knew this was the moment that mattered. How I reacted to this question was going to determine my future. Everything depended on whether my body said yes or no to this question. What I said with my mouth didn't matter. My body's reactions were what mattered, and I certainly couldn't control my body's reactions. I knew that every measurement of my body was going to spike and say yes every time he asked the question.

"Did you, at any time, sexually touch or fondle or kiss James Evans for your own sexual pleasure?"

My body flushed with fear. Angry and helpless, I responded, "No." I looked at Mr. Paolella and said, "I know my whole body just said yes even though I said no."

"Mr. Kraemer, we're going to do this several times. Just relax and answer the questions. Did you, at any time, sexually touch or fondle or kiss James Evans for your own sexual pleasure?"

"No." Again, my body did the same thing.

"Did you offer or force James Evans to take any unlawful drugs?"

"No."

"Did you threaten James Evans or his family if he told of anything that supposedly transpired at the mission agency where you work?"

"No."

"Did you sexually abuse any of the other children in the mission agency?"

"No."

With each question, my body flushed with fear. Mr. Paolella released the blood pressure monitor on my arm and said, "Mr. Kraemer, we're going to do this again. I am going to leave the room for a while and will return in a few minutes."

With that, he left, and I remained seated, still hooked up to the monitors, and stared at the wall ahead of me. Before my eyes, I imagined Jesus hanging on the cross, helpless, incapable of doing anything to change his situation. I begged him to help me. I cried and pleaded with him to make me relax enough to pass this test. After several minutes of crying and praying, I realized there was nothing I could do. I had to trust God, let go of everything, and accept my situation, even if I was wrongfully found guilty.

Mr. Paolella returned to the room and repeated everything as before, with what I felt were exactly the same results. With each question, my body flushed with fear, although I was becoming more comfortable with the reality that there was nothing I could do but accept the process.

When we finished, Mr. Paolella said we were going to do this one last time, and again he would first leave the room for a few minutes. I was sure this was because I was failing. I was still frightened but was beginning to feel more of a passive acceptance about the situation rather than a fighting self-preservation. When he returned, he repeated his questions, and we were done. He told me he would contact Kim Adams within a week. I was too afraid to ask questions, so I walked out silently. I cried all the way home.

When I arrived back at the mission agency about an hour later, Kim Adams was outside the building where her office was located. She asked me how things had gone. I told her I thought I had failed the exam—my body had kept saying I was guilty even though I was innocent. She assured me that if I had failed the polygraph exam, the four-member panel was determined to do whatever they needed, and spend whatever was needed, to establish my innocence. If I failed the polygraph test, they would send me to a forensic psychologist in Bakersfield by the name of Dr. Dean Haddock, an expert in criminal profiles who would be able to establish that my personality did not fit that of a liar and sexual perpetrator.

I meekly thanked Kim and made my way up to my own office. I called my biological dad and told him what had happened. While we were still talking about it, a second call came in. Kim Adams was on the second line. With excitement, she said, "Brian, you passed the polygraph test! Mr. Paolella just called and said that he and several of his associates met with you, and they all agree you are telling the truth." I cried with joy and relief. Kim and I said good-bye, and I went back to my dad. With joy, I told him the good news, and we were both very relieved. Now what would be the next step? Would I still be evaluated by Dr. Haddock in Bakersfield?

21

Preparing for the Weekend with Tim

On Saturday, March 21, I went to Tim's home for a "Moving Out of the House" party. Linda and Stuart were there, and I met Tim's adopted daughter, Susan, for the first time. She seemed normal even though Tim had told me she had multiple personalities. I felt awkward because I was used to having Tim all to myself and spending almost all of our time cuddling and talking, but he was busy with various tasks, including interacting with everyone, helping get food ready, and all sorts of fatherly responsibilities.

Tim, Linda, and Stuart were moving in with Tim's spiritual brother, Paul, and his two boys. I asked him if I could help him move the following weekend. This would allow me to stay overnight again on that Friday, March 27. He accepted my offer, and I looked forward to talking to him about the details on Wednesday.

On Wednesday, I found myself feeling angry because our time together had become little more than the two of us cuddling on the couch, with me talking about whatever was on my mind and Tim nodding off, probably because his level of Zoloft was too high. I was beginning to think Tim didn't care enough about me to stay awake. Our conversation was minimal, and many times he didn't even follow what I was saying.

Our boundaries were relaxed again during our sessions in his office. A couple weeks had passed since Dr. Ashman admonished him to be more cautious and aware of my sexual arousal. Tim allowed me to unbutton his shirt, run my hands all over his chest, take my own shirt off, and lean against him skin to skin. In my mind, this was innocent enough because it was merely a son exploring and being close to his father, and I didn't feel guilty because I had already told Dr. Ashman what was happening. There were no secrets. After all, it was Tim's responsibility to set the boundaries. I was his little boy. He was my dad, and he was certainly smart enough to know how to raise me.

It seems foolish now, exceptionally foolish, that we could believe we were anything but two hot-blooded men needy for physical affection and same-sex intimacy. We were both strong Christians, and we believed it sinful to be homosexual. The need to believe oneself to be innocent causes deeply religious people to become geniuses at justification and rationalization.

Tim shared with me in one of these counseling sessions that he had alter personalities, but I didn't need to be afraid because he was aware of them, and "the children" rarely "came out"—he spoke of his alter egos as "the children." He had received a lot of care from Dr. Ashman, and his dissociative issues were under control, so he was capable of being a good husband and father and therapist. I found the idea frightening. How could I be sure that one of Tim's alter personalities wouldn't come out in our time together? Would he use a different voice? Would he remember he was my spiritual father? Would he recognize me or be some completely different person? This was not what I had wanted when I got into this relationship.

That same day, I was nervous and excited about our plans for Friday and Saturday. I was going to sleep overnight on Friday. I knew that my ultimate goal was to be physically naked with Tim and yet not have sex. I imagined a naked little infant falling asleep on his father's chest as one of the most beautiful and innocent experiences possible. There could be no greater safety or security than that level of connection. This was my route to wholeness, to start again as an innocent baby with a perfect father. It seems crazy now, but it made sense to me at the time, and it seemed to make sense to Tim as well. I was sure that once I had this level of intimacy with him, I would stop needing him so much. After all, healthy people grow up and don't cling to their parents like when they were babies.

I wanted to let Tim know what I was hoping for and to present it in such a way that he would likely agree with me. Of course, I also wanted him to be smart enough to say no if it was a poor idea.

That evening, I sent him another e-mail. In it, I shared a lengthy, rambling, and pleading letter I had written that day to God.

> Dear God,
>
> I like the skin contact with Dad. I like to take my shirt off and I like it when he takes his shirt off and we put our skin together. I like to rub his back and caress his tummy and pull his beard and his ears and his moustache and rub his face with the back of my hand. I like it when he puts his hand on my bottom and massages me there. I like it when he says, "I love you" and "You're really easy to love" and "I'm so glad you're my son" and "I enjoy being with you" and all those other nice things he says.
>
> As far as I can see, it appears that my Dad is all mine. Every bit of him is mine. I think I'm probably going to be able to be naked with him if that is what I want. I like the possibility, but I'm not sure if I'm more scared to have the option or be denied the option. I can imagine myself lying in bed with Dad, both completely naked, holding one another, me thinking, "This is wonderful, but am I healed yet? Am I able now to relax and feel totally accepted and safe? Am I able to feel like Dad and I are one, or am I going to still feel distant and maybe even afraid that we've done a bad thing by being naked together?"
>
> God, I don't want Dad to hold back from me. Part of my aching is to know I am truly his boy, his son, his man, his little one, his child, his little self developing into a man. I need to know my Daddy is available to me in every way but sin. God, help him be wise regarding what is sin. Help him to know what I need and to be able to give that to me and to know what would be harmful and to say no to that. His role is much harder than mine. I am still a child in many ways and I'm taking advantage of the opportunity to just be me, not judging myself too much or putting too many holds on myself.
>
> If I want to see Dad naked, I will probably just ask, "Dad, can we hold each other naked?" What boldness! What lack of fear! What courage! But God, I only have such courage because I trust you

are in control of both of us. I know the damage sexual sin can do to a man. Please help us be totally close and totally righteous at the same time.

I trust that when Dad and I have completely connected, then my own masculinity, my manhood, my power, strength, energy, will come bubbling up and desire to be expressed in relationship with a woman. The second cannot come without the first.

I ache inside for Dad. I want to be next to him all the time. Will you please help me quit feeling sexually aroused when I'm next to him? It's very uncomfortable having a penis that feels aroused constantly, even just thinking about being close to him.

God, our intimacy depends upon you. We need your presence always. We need you to go to bed with us up at that cabin on May 15. I hope that you will not allow Dad to be overwhelmed by his son's thoughts. There are so many ways I fear I will drive him away. I don't ever want to lose him. Will this longing go away after a while? Will it intensify? Will it lessen? As we get even physically more intensely close, will that increase or decrease the longing?

Your son,

Brian

It is obvious to me now that I was repeating the same themes I had obsessed on since childhood. What I really needed at this point was medicine, not more analysis. My brain was out of control. My serotonin levels were out of whack, but it would be several years more before I would find this out. For now I wrestled a thousand times with my thoughts and feelings, and I believe Tim did his best to try to be a source of comfort. It seems odd, though, that Tim, being a marriage and family therapist, didn't see the obvious signs of an ongoing obsessive-compulsive nature that could have been mitigated with medication.

22

CROSSING THE LINE

On Friday afternoon, I arrived at Tim's home to help him pack, hold a garage sale Saturday morning, and move his stuff Saturday afternoon, but my main goal was to be as intimate with Tim as possible without crossing the line of being sexual. Linda and Stuart were already at the new home shared with Paul and his boys. I was going to be alone with Tim all night.

Tim wanted to go for a drive around the city and visit a bookstore. He was far more interested in looking at books than I was. I wanted to get home and cuddle. I followed him around while he looked at various titles. Suddenly, he opened the pages of a book to me, and there staring me in the face was a page of naked men having sex. I recoiled in fear and disgust. With vehement grief, my voice quavering with emotion, I protested, "I didn't want to see that!" I felt betrayed by this man I called Dad.

I had not looked at pornography since my religious conversion in May 1984. I was happy that I had made the choice to walk away from homosexuality and everything associated with it. For nearly fourteen years, I had not looked at a naked photo of a man or woman or any form of pornography. I was horrified that my own dad would violate me in this way, especially given that he was supposed to be helping me become heterosexual, not tempting me to be homosexual. I looked away from him and resentfully followed him silently until we got to the car.

"What's wrong, son?" he asked once we were inside the car.

With anger bordering on rage and eyes filled with tears, I said, "Dad, I haven't looked at pornography for thirteen years, and you put it in my face. You didn't even ask me. You just forced me to look at it. I can't believe you did that!" I again looked away from him as my eyes overflowed with tears. I cried, and he put his arms around me and said how sorry he was; he only wanted me to not be so hung up about things and so worried about everything, he said. He was trying to help me have a more carefree, relaxed attitude about my life and thought it would be funny, not a violation of my innocence.

As we drove home, I was silent for a while, thinking about how my thirteen-year record was broken and couldn't be fixed. But I could just think of it as a brief thing that had been forced on me, that I hadn't chosen, and therefore my purity was still intact. As we neared the house, I knew that if I wanted to feel close to Tim, I was going to have to forgive him and move on with our relationship. I still wanted to cuddle with him.

It seems ironic as I consider the disconnect between my anxiety over seeing naked men having sex and my own fascination with being naked with Tim—my fierce determination to remain morally "pure" while simultaneously pushing every boundary in my developing physical relationship with Tim. I was also pushing boundaries of nudity at home with my six male housemates. I insisted on being nude when walking between my bedroom and our bathroom, even if I had a morning erection, and of course, I hiked nude in the mountains above our home. I had an immovable belief system that didn't allow me to be homosexual. By thinking of myself as an innocent child exploring his father, I could rationalize my every behavior, no matter how arousing and provocative.

That night, we pushed two single mattresses side by side on the floor. I, as always, was naked, and Tim, as usual, was wearing only his boxer shorts. We lay holding one another and caressing and stroking each other for hours. As before, we touched each other everywhere with the exception of the penis, scrotum, and anus. Anything else was available because it was only sensual and not sexual by our definitions.

Early Saturday morning, perhaps 1:00 a.m. or later, after massaging Tim's chest and arms and belly, I moved ever closer and closer to his pubic region. I was determined to get as close to his penis as I could without touching it. To touch his penis would have been sexual. To touch anything else was only sensual and therefore okay. Finally, I put my fingers barely into his pubic hair, just above his penis. I did not want to touch his penis or his scrotum, but I did want to get as close as I possibly could in order to feel like nothing was being denied me and like I was able to be completely intimate with him without being sexual, as we were defining it.

Then something happened that I didn't expect. He moved his fingers down my stomach and into my pubic hair and began massaging me in the same way I was massaging him. This frightened me. Why would a father want to massage his son in his pubic region? What I was doing was okay because I was the child exploring his father (a major rationalization), but what he was doing to me was wrong. His actions were obviously sexual, and this made me feel sick and scared inside. I could understand my wanting to be close to him and my wanting to "explore" my dad, but the other way around didn't make any sense, and I felt frightened, like I was being molested all over again, this time by my spiritual dad. I was also afraid of whether I was going to be able to forgive him for what certainly felt like being molested. He fell asleep, and I tossed and turned all night.

Morning came, and I spent Sunday as planned, helping Tim hold the garage sale and move out of one house and into his spiritual brother's house. I also brought up a subject I had been thinking about for quite a while. I felt awkward paying Tim for therapy since paying him took away from the experience of being his son. A son wouldn't pay his dad for therapy. I had long ago stopped thinking of our times together as counseling appointments. I was Tim's son, and I wanted to hang out with Dad at his work. I explained how I saw things, and Tim agreed that would be fine. I would no longer pay him for counseling.

23

Why Did He Do It?

On Monday, March 30, while in his office, I asked Tim why he had put his fingers in my pubic hair and massaged me there on Friday night. He said he didn't remember doing that. I insisted he had, and he said he couldn't argue with me, but he simply didn't remember doing it. I was disturbed by his unwillingness or inability to remember this, and I wondered whether he had been in one of his alters when he had done it and was unable to access that memory. It frightened me that he could be doing things without awareness. I was terribly frightened that I had been molested by Tim; how would I get over this and forgive him and move on with our relationship? I needed him to be a good man. I needed him to be a safe, secure, heterosexual man who loved his wife and was going to help me be heterosexual. I wanted a safe daddy, not a homosexual dad with alter personalities who found me sexually arousing. Mostly, I was frightened of losing him.

Because of Tim's putting his fingers in my pubic hair, each time he said something complimentary, I wanted to say something angry and sarcastic back. When he said something such as "I really like you!" I thought, *I bet you do!* It was difficult, but I wanted to tell him everything I was thinking, so I even told him my angry, sarcastic thoughts in response to his seeming endearments. He listened as I expressed my anger, but he continued to go in and out of being half-asleep, apologizing for being so sleepy. Dr. Nicolosi (1991), knowing the potential hazards of the therapeutic relationship, wrote,

The therapist needs to be able to hold in check an overly seductive client, who may stir up feelings in him which he fears may be sexual (whether or not, in fact, they are). If the therapist permits a sexual encounter, needless to say the consequences will be devastating to the client. After an initial period of short-term gratification and excitement, the client will lose his ability to trust and will feel used and exploited; the therapeutic relationship will be destroyed, and the client will become cynical about all psychotherapy. (p. 182)

On Tuesday morning, I faxed a letter to Dr. Ashman and asked to meet with him again. I let him know that I was no longer going to be paying Tim as a therapist, that I had stayed overnight with Tim on Friday, and that I needed to talk with him privately about similar things we had discussed before.

On Wednesday, April 1, I had my usual appointment with Tim. During the course of this appointment, he acknowledged putting his fingers in my pubic hair and massaging me there, but he couldn't explain why he had done it. This frightened me; I was becoming very angry at the thought that he was using me sexually. That morning, as we were cuddling on his couch, he said, "It's really easy to love you." I thought silently, *Of course it is! You're using me sexually and telling me how easy it easy to enjoy me!*

We spent the whole appointment, like the majority of our times together, lying on the couch, semi-reclined, as I massaged his arms and chest. In spite of my wariness about him possibly using me sexually, I still wanted to be physically close to him. As usual, he apologized for being tired and said the Zoloft was making him sleepy. I didn't want to wake him since I wasn't paying him anything for these appointments anymore.

On Thursday, I met with Dr. Ashman and went over a handwritten list of questions and concerns.

1. Can I trust Dad that his own sexual issues aren't going to get in the way of him loving me in a wholesome way?
2. What is a reasonable expectation of "healing" given my relationship with Dad? What does "healing" of homosexual and homoemotional feelings mean?
3. Is it okay for Dad to see me naked, me him, shower together, touch each other all over? How are boundaries established? Aren't we two hot-blooded men who could too easily be fornicating?

4. Is there really a clear difference between sexual and "closeness between father and son" (sensual), or are we playing games with words to justify our behavior?
5. Fathers and sons don't normally run their hands all over each other. This desire is abnormal. If fulfilled, will the desire lessen or increase?

At the bottom of my list, I wrote the word *gratitude* to remind myself to make sure to convey this attitude to Dr. Ashman, who I was fairly sure was feeling anxiety about the relationship between Tim and me and who might be tempted to bring it to an end.

Late into the session, with exasperation I said, "Bill, I just can't get over this issue about the pubic hair."

Dr. Ashman said, "Brian, why are you having such difficulty just admitting that your dad sexually abused you?" He was referring to Tim.

I said, "I'm so glad you said that because that's what I believe too. I just need to admit it in order to get over it and go on."

As before, I felt completely safe when talking with Dr. Ashman. He was a wise and caring professional. I felt much safer with him than I did with Tim now. The only physical contact I had with Dr. Ashman was a somewhat awkward and brief hug I initiated before parting. He commended me for the depth of insight of my questions and said I was more aware and insightful on these issues than my spiritual dad. He was disappointed with how poorly Tim was handling things. I could tell he was frustrated, maybe even angry, and it was likely Tim was going to be reprimanded by Dr. Ashman for his reckless behavior Friday night.

I was relieved Dr. Ashman did not say that Tim and I needed to stop being father and son or stop spending time together, but he repeated his previous warnings: I must tell Tim every detail of when I felt aroused or uncomfortable or afraid. He also said if I was concerned about anything and wanted to talk with him again, about anything at all, he would like to meet with me.

That night, I wrote an e-mail to Tim letting him know about my meeting with Dr. Ashman and warning him that Dr. Ashman might want to talk with him because he didn't think Tim was being careful enough in his spiritual fathering of me. I said, "I just want you to know I love you so you don't get upset with me. I wasn't trying to get you in trouble, just understand my feelings better and understand you better."

Within a week or two of seeing the nude photos at the bookstore with Tim, I could contain my desire for more no longer. I used a computer in my office at the mission agency to do a search for "nude men," "naked men," "gay men," "gay hunks," and whatever else I could think of. There seemed to be no limit to the amount of homosexual pornography available. I began spending hours in my office every day looking at these photos, and I feared getting caught.

I repeatedly felt guilty and made resolutions and promises to God and myself to stop. I chose a password that used the letters F, S, H, and S, which stood for Father, Son, and Holy Spirit, figuring that having to "step over" the Father, Son, and Holy Spirit every time I accessed pornography might help me to resist it. In reality, I just became comfortable stepping over the Trinity.

24

James Confesses He Lied

Since January 30, 1998, the four-member panel had been working diligently to prove my innocence in the allegations made against me by James Evans. They reached their conclusions on April 3, 1998, and I was told soon thereafter that I had been found innocent and that, in fact, James had now confessed to lying about the molestations. Upon being told, I cried tears of relief and anger.

The previous nine weeks had been the worst of my adult life. When I think about the period between when I was accused and when I was exonerated, it feels like it lasted six months. I was surprised when reviewing the documents to find that in fact it was only a nine-week period, but my exaggerated memory of the time frame demonstrates how stressful and frightening it was for me.

I was asked to meet with the four members of the committee that had worked so diligently to establish my innocence as well as the founder of our mission agency, Dr. Rudolph Clemens, grandfather of James. We sat around a large circular table, and I felt like a little boy surrounded by my protectors. I think they felt a great deal of compassion and sorrow for me. The executive director, Leonard Billings, the man who had assured me from the first day of this horror that he would trust me with his own children, stood up and began to read the following letter from James's father. As he read, I quietly sobbed throughout, never once looking up from the table.

May 22, 1998

Dear Brian and Committee,

I want to thank you as a committee for investing your valuable time in pursuing this matter of James's claims on our behalf, and in doing it with such great discretion and personal concern for both parties. Your ability to regard our feelings and personal anguish as it relates to James made it much easier for us to trust all involved in overseeing this process.

I want to particularly address Brian with this letter, but to do so in the context of the committee. I hope that a phone call can also help us reconcile matters on a more private basis, Brian, and we hope for an opportunity for future face to face communication. But we originally asked that a committee be assigned to investigate these matters, and I believe it's appropriate for them to hear our personal conclusions towards you.

Brian, as you already know, James has confessed to fabricating lies which implicated you in abusing him while we were in southern California from 1995 to 1997. We were able to establish this through the skillful intervention of a social worker trained in obtaining these kinds of testimonies here in Australia. Either in confusion relating to his emotional and psychological difficulties stemming from past abuse, his chronic disabilities, his overmedicated mental state, or simply from a sinful act of personal retribution or manipulative behavior, James has wrongfully charged you with abusing him. Let it be clear that we hold no further charge against you, Brian, but only regret that we have caused you tremendous personal agony throughout this investigation.

As James's father I must also take certain responsibility for proceeding at this level of investigation. It was undertaken with great reluctance, but the need to understand the source of my son's personal problems, and the potential harm that might have been happening in a community we both value very highly, overruled any final hesitancy. I had been advised by legal counsel of the potential fabrication by abuse victims like James. I was alternatively advised by four psychologists as to what action should be taken. Having been betrayed years ago by a missionary friend who indulged in sadistic abuse of my son, I must admit that I have been more easily suspicious of those who seem to act with integrity in the Christian ministry.

I want you, Brian, to understand my heartfelt remorse that you have been dragged through this humiliating process. While you are not the first person who has been hurt as a result of James's difficulties, you are probably the one most personally exposed and thoroughly examined. Your personal integrity and willing graciousness has allowed it to take place at such personal cost to yourself. I appeal to these same Godly qualities, Brian, in asking your forgiveness for whatever pain I, as James's father, have caused you in this pursuit.

I want the committee to determine whether there is any further amends needed in seeing this investigation to a successful conclusion. I want you to feel free, Brian, if there were any damaging references to your personhood outside the committee, to please let us know what we can do to clear your name and reputation in the eyes of all. While we know you may feel that this process may have compromised our relationship, we will do whatever we can to see that your reputation is not compromised with anyone else.

Again, thank you, committee members, for the investment of yourselves in this effort. Each one of you has expended more than time in seeing that our family, and James in particular, receives a certain attention as to these claims, and in such a compassionate way.

In Him,

Harold Evans

My nightmare of being accused of molesting a child was over, but at what a cost! I now feared children in a way I never had before. I did not feel safe being affectionate with them. I imagined that other people suspected me of being a child molester. I was even hesitant to look at them, play with them, or show interest in them.

Eight years later, I was still bothered by the question, why did James accuse me? I wrote to Harold and asked if he had any further insight to answer this.

He responded, "You weren't the only one accused as James fabricated his way through his post-traumatic stress." His parents believed that he was molested while they were missionaries in Algeria. He continued, "Other missionaries were accused of sexual misconduct by James, and they too went through a degree of examination. You were Ahmed's roommate and by association could have been drawn into everything. James fabricated the details of the inside of your house and this inaccuracy is what led to his charges being judged as fabricated." My roommate, Ahmed, was from Algeria, and though he had an innocent friendship with James, Harold suspects his son may have found it triggering because of alleged past sexual abuse from a male in that country.

Closing this chapter of my life, I wrote back to Harold,

> I appreciate you taking the time to answer my question and I want you to know I do not have lingering anger toward you or Tonya or James. I am happy to hear James is doing better now. I no longer judge him or condemn him or even feel the slightest bit of anger toward him, for I know that, like the rest of us, his choices were greatly influenced by the many particulars of his internal and external situation, particulars likely painful and difficult and which I cannot begin to appreciate or understand. I know you and Tonya and the family have suffered incomparably more than those of us momentarily drawn into the situation. I sincerely wish the best for all of you and particularly James. I would welcome communication with you and your family at any time. I truly feel relieved that we can talk like this.

25

Overnight at Tim's New House and the Cabin

On Saturday, April 18, I stayed overnight at Tim's new house, the one he and his family now shared with his spiritual brother, Paul, and Paul's two sons, Gabriel and David. Linda was gone to a women's retreat. Paul was an attractive man with a handsome face and a sculpted body from working out. There was a photo of him shirtless, displaying a perfect set of abdominal muscles, on the refrigerator door. I could see why Tim was drawn to him as a spiritual brother, and it seemed to me that Tim's attraction to Paul was more than brotherly kindness. It seemed he probably had some kind of a crush on Paul like I had on him. In fact, Tim seemed needy around Paul, as if he was looking to Paul to satisfy some kind of emptiness he felt, like I looked to him to satisfy my longings.

Looking back, I believe Tim's attraction to Paul was fundamentally sexual. He admired his physique, his good looks, his confidence with women, and his boyish charm and humor. Paul likely appreciated the admiration he received from Tim and enjoyed being friends with a respected therapist. Paul worked with his hands, and Tim worked with his mind.

All afternoon, I thought about where I was going to sleep. Would I sleep with Tim, or would he want to sleep with Paul? Again, because Linda was gone, I had a feeling that Tim was going to want to sleep with Paul. That night, Tim fixed up a second single bed in his room so that I could sleep in the same room with him. As we lay in our two beds, I told him that I was curious about what his penis looked like and wanted to see it. He asked me why, and I assured him it was only because I was curious. He pulled back the blankets and pulled down his boxers enough for me to see his flaccid penis. I asked if I could touch it and promised I wasn't going to do anything to it. He said it was okay. I poked it with my index finger. He was not aroused. I did not find his penis attractive, but seeing it satisfied my curiosity and made me feel close to him, not separated in any way. He trusted me enough to even let me touch his penis. I had no interest in arousing him. With my curiosity satiated, we cuddled like we usually did, and I went to sleep.

The reader may be asking, "What the hell were you thinking, asking him if you could see and touch his penis? How in the world did you think this was going to help you go straight? It seems like the opposite of your goals for yourself and the opposite of his goals for you." I agree it seems crazy, but I didn't think it was, and I still don't think it was. I wanted to satisfy my curiosity so that I could get over it. I figured that seeing his penis would take away my curiosity, and that is what it did. I admit my reaction may have been different if I had found his penis attractive. In that case, I don't know what my reaction would have been. By asking him if I could touch it, I was pushing the boundaries of my freedom. I'm glad he let me. I wasn't trying to arouse him. In fact, I didn't want to arouse him. I wanted to fulfill my compulsion to touch him.

Again, my behavior can be understood only in light of my brain chemistry. A year and a half earlier, in December 1996, at age thirty-three, I had been diagnosed by a psychiatrist as having had obsessive-compulsive disorder (OCD) as a child. I no longer met the criteria for the diagnosis as an adult, but the psychiatrist told me I had a classic case of OCD as a child and teenager. If Tim would have gotten aroused, I would have been bothered. If Tim had refused to show me his penis, I would have been bothered. If Tim had refused to let me touch his penis, I would have been bothered. This level of trust and availability made me feel close to him.

On Friday, May 15, Tim and I went on a cabin retreat together northeast of Castaic Lake Recreational Area near Lake Hughes. A missionary couple from our agency had a beautiful home there and permitted our staff members to use it for a nominal fee. There wasn't much to do there, but being physically close to Tim was all I wanted. I had been looking forward to this trip for a long time.

After checking out the area and getting settled, I asked whether we could take a shower together. I thought of this as being okay because I was "Dad's little boy," and showering together would be a natural experience for father and son. Tim agreed it would be fine, although it was a rather confined space for both of us. I knew I would get aroused, but I was disappointed when Tim did as well. I asked him why this had happened, and he said he didn't know. I feared he was aroused because he was sexually attracted to me, and I did not want that to be true. If he was sexually attracted to me, that would threaten everything about our relationship.

That night, we slept in a queen-size bed and massaged each other as usual, avoiding the genitals. At one point during the evening, my penis went flaccid, and I proudly displayed it to Tim. This was my goal, to be physically intimate with Tim without being sexually aroused. I was happy I was making progress. The next day, we left the cabin around noon and returned to his and Paul's home.

26

Dissociative Alter Egos or Childish Role-Playing?

I was grateful for my spiritual dad but also had high expectations of his time and attention. Although it was unrealistic, I wanted to be treated exactly as his other biological and spiritual children. If this father–son relationship was real, then I should be able to expect everything any child would expect. I hesitated to demand things, but I didn't hesitate to choose my words carefully and attempt to get what I wanted. I had planned on spending the upcoming Memorial Day with Tim and his family, but things were not working out as I expected. Tim said I wasn't going to be able to join them and suggested Paul didn't want me to be included, and it was his house.

Early on Sunday morning, May 24, I wrote a pleading e-mail to Tim:

> I want you to get a home where I can always come, no matter what. In my mind, I never moved away from home so I don't think I should need special permission to come home now. I have not "moved away from home" in my heart yet. I'm not "old enough" to do that yet. Please don't make me act "older" than I am in my heart. I don't take up much space and I can be really quiet. This may sound like a little kid, but that's how I feel in my heart. I feel like your little boy who needs to promise "I don't take up much space and I can be really quiet" to show you how much I want to be with you. I'm not a distant relative that gets invited over once in awhile. I am your son. My heart feels at home when I'm with

you and Linda. Please work something out. I don't want Paul to be mad, though. I love you, Daddy.

Your boy,

Brian

An hour later, I called Tim. I was crying when he answered the phone. I was angry, and I pleaded with him, using guilt and whatever else I could think of to try to get him to change his mind about letting me join him for Memorial Day. I felt justified in behaving like a child because I believed I was a child. I might have been a thirty-four-year-old adult, but I was also a child, and until I got past being a child, I was determined to be my true self. It was Tim's responsibility to provide me with guidance and boundaries.

I hurt inside so much that I was lying on the floor rolling around in pain as I talked with him. I also felt terribly divided up mentally. Sometimes the intensity of my feelings frightened me, as they did on that Sunday morning. Tim had talked about his own experience of dissociation, referring to his alter egos, some little kid alters and others more mature, but still distinct and powerful in personality. I feared that perhaps I was dissociative as well, especially when I permitted myself to behave in such a pleading, desperate, childish way.

I discussed this with him at times, but we hadn't decided whether I had alter egos like he did. We used language such as "adult parts" and "child parts." I didn't want to believe I was dissociative because in my mind that represented a much deeper level of mental illness than I believed myself to have. I assured myself I did not have full-blown multiple personality disorder because I did not have blank spots in my memory or lapses in events. I was very conscious of everything I was feeling at all times, whether I was behaving as a mature thirty-four-year-old or as an angry child.

At the same time, I was trying to make sense of the intensity of my conflicted feelings and began to adopt his understanding of dissociation as my own. This particular morning, I felt frightened by my fractured sense of self. One voice pleaded with Tim while another voice laughed at me, saying, "This is ridiculous. Pull yourself together and be normal again." Another part simply watched everything and tried to make sense out of it. I felt like if I was coming unraveled emotionally and like perhaps my "parts" were all coming forward at the same time, not running away from each other or hiding from each other, as I heard happened in MPD. I thought, "I don't want to have multiple personality disorder. This can't be true. This is terrible." At the same time, I thought, "Perhaps this is progress. Maybe my 'parts' feel safe enough with Tim to finally come forward together."

Tim listened to me, and once I calmed down, we said good-bye. He didn't invite me to join the family, but I was sure he would talk to Paul and tell him how much I needed to be with him, and Paul would change his mind. All day, I waited for the call. I was afraid that if I didn't get to go, I would withdraw into myself and hide the parts of my personality again. It didn't seem fair for my little child to reveal himself so openly only to be told his dad didn't have time to be with him. I felt abandoned and had to fend for myself.

I knew I could probably pull myself together, let my adult parts express themselves, and ignore the kid part, but the thought frightened me. The kid part would have to pretend to be together until the following Wednesday. I would have to go to work all day on Tuesday and be an adult. It seemed like an interminable time to wait for a child.

Looking back on this, I am amazed I took this role-playing so seriously, but I can understand how it happened. None of us are just the age we are at the moment, but we are an accumulation of every experience we've ever had. I wasn't just a thirty-four-year-old adult professional that Sunday morning. I was also an academic twenty-five-year-old, a lusty seventeen-year-old, an inquisitive nine-year-old, a pouting two-year-old, and every other aspect of my life's experiences. I was every thought, action, intention, and experience of my life, and I could call forth any part of it, depending on the circumstances. Tim and I were operating in a therapeutic model that encouraged me to think of myself as a child, and that is what I did. I took the model seriously and interpreted all of my experiences in light of that model.

I now think it was foolish to believe I was expressing dissociative identity disorder. Tim and several of his fellow therapists at Christ's Counseling Center specialized in this, and to a hammer, everything looks like a nail. It seems to me that Tim, without intending to, added to my distress by suggesting I might be dissociative like he thought himself to be. I was trying to make sense out of my feelings. This was one way of interpreting my behavior. I think it was an unfortunate one.

That evening, Tim wrote me:

I'm glad we got to talk on the phone this morning. I am sorry that you are feeling so sad about not being able to come out. I feel a little irresponsible for bringing it up in the first place. Let me say a little more about needing to feel like you can come here any time without a special invitation. Son, you are family and anywhere I live is your home. Of course, a child never needs permission to come and go from their parent's home. However, part of you is an adult. Adult children recognize that their parents have other needs and responsibilities and in fact are not always available. None of my children (including Carla or Stuart when he gets older) could count on us always being available or free to be with them whenever they wanted to come over. If Carla lives in the same town or near us after college, she will need to call to see if we're home or if we have other plans before she drops by ... We will not be available for her 24 hours a day. I know your adult parts understand this. But a little boy cannot understand his parents not being available at any time ... which makes sense. If you were in a crisis and needed me, the things I need to do on Monday would naturally disappear as unimportant. But that is not the case and I do need to be responsible with my time. I love you and I love spending time with you, and I'm sure I will be sad a part of the time on Monday that you're not with us. But I do have a lot I need to do. And, I need to spend some time with Linda. Stuart went to a friend's house for a sleepover so we will have the morning together (if the boys will leave us alone). Anyway, I hope this helps. But it may not ... just remember you can always talk to me about whatever you're feeling, and you will never get in trouble with me for anything you say or feel. I will talk to you later.

Love,

Dad

Still later, I responded,

> I can understand this thing about my adult parts having to understand and my child parts having a hard time understanding. I hope I didn't make you mad at me tonight by being so demanding. I really do love and need you. Your love for me is so meaningful and I'm still afraid of losing you. Please don't let my demanding and ungrateful attitude make you change your mind about liking me. Please never stop telling me you love me. I need to hear it over and over and over and over. Thank you, Dad. Good night. I love you.
>
> Your son and boy,
>
> Brian

On Memorial Day afternoon, Tim wrote,

> I did not see what was happening to you Sunday morning as dramatic as you were experiencing it. I am so used to dissociative behavior that it seems normal to me! And we had talked about you being a little boy before, and there have been times when you sounded like and acted like a child, so to me it was not that new. But obviously you were feeling it on a deeper level of awareness than ever before. I know exactly how that feels and how scary it can be! I am sorry you felt abandoned. You are not. Dad loves you. I am committed to you. I will *never* criticize or shame you for your feelings, or for being a little boy. I love all the different parts of you and you need all of them. The parts you most dislike or are uncomfortable with are the parts that need redeeming the most. It is very hard when the little boys are out and I have to "talk over their heads" to the adult parts ... especially hard knowing the little boys cannot possibly understand what I'm doing or why. And there is not enough history for them to be able to say, "But I know this dad. He won't hurt me. He will be back." I understand that. I wish there was a way for all of this to be painless, but there is not, not that I've found.

I survived waiting until Wednesday, and we discussed my experience during our counseling session. Though I was using dissociative terms such as "adult parts" and "child parts," I was not comfortable adopting the label of multiple personality disorder. It seemed more reasonable to me that we are all complicated people with conflicting thoughts and emotions, and the voices I was hearing were merely my own brain capable of thinking a lot of varied ideas at once. Now I believe that applying this alter ego talk to my own conflicted feelings was wrong. It was confusing and harmful and came out of my own therapist's identity issues rather than an accurate diagnosis of my own.

According to the *Diagnostic and Statistical Manual of Mental Disorders* (4th ed., text rev., 2000), "Dissociative Identity Disorder (formerly Multiple Personality Disorder) is characterized by the presence of two or more distinct identities or personality states that recurrently take control of the individual's behavior accompanied by an inability to recall important personal information that is too extensive to be explained by ordinary forgetfulness." This disorder was popularized in the 1957 film *The Three Faces of Eve* and later in *Sybil*, a 1976 film starring Sally Field. The latter film was remade and released in 2007 with Tammy Blanchard as Sybil Dorsett. All of this is to say, I did not have the symptoms of this severe mental disorder and never should have suffered the experience of thinking I might. My therapist had interpreted his own behavior using this model, had adopted this mental illness as his own, and unfortunately tried to apply it to me.

27

More Counseling Sessions

E ach Monday and Wednesday as I drove from my home to Tim's office in San Fernando, I found myself sexually aroused in anticipation of being held by him. I considered it part of the process of learning to separate sexual from sensual, a distinction I no longer maintain. It's obvious to me now that I found our time together sexually stimulating and more indicative of a lovers' relationship than a parent–child one, though I refused to believe that at the time.

Some of our conversations were about a new woman I was dating named Veronica Dickerson. She worked at our mission agency and was from Dominica, one of the Caribbean Islands. The first day we had lunch together, I told her, "I need to warn you. I break women's hearts. I used to be gay, and I still struggle with homosexual feelings." This didn't seem to bother her. In the weeks and months ahead, she formed relationships with other women online who were married to men who struggled with homosexual feelings. She was determined to do everything she could to help me in my search for sexual and emotional healing.

She cooked for me all the time and made delicious and nutritious meals. I held her and enjoyed the softness of her arms. They were very different than men's arms. I never hesitated to make comments about how attractive I found particular men. Our friendship was based on honesty. Though I held her and stroked her arms, I never felt sexually aroused by her.

In our sessions, Tim shared more and more about his own struggles as I shared mine. He revealed that he was tempted to look at gay porn on the computer, that he communicated with gay men online, and that he even met some occasionally. He provided free counseling for gay and bisexual men on the Internet on Sunday nights from 6:00 to 9:00 p.m. He would sometimes exchange phone numbers and develop relationships with some of these men. I'm sure he encouraged many men to be faithful to their wives and girlfriends, but I was also concerned about the safety of his forming friendships with gay men over the Internet and how that might threaten our family and our relationship as father and son.

He told me about an African American man back east whom he had met online. They found each other attractive, and when Tim was in Pennsylvania visiting Andy, his most recent spiritually adopted son, he made a detour to visit this man as well. Another gay man he met online offered to give him a massage. I don't know whether he accepted it, but I do remember feeling frightened that he could be tempted to be sexual with the man, and this could potentially destroy our family. I felt he was playing with fire and endangering all of us in the process.

Another time, he told me about a friend online who received a photograph from a coworker that showed him ejaculating. I was grossed out and asked him to not tell me things like this. I couldn't see why he would put such a disgusting image in my mind.

28

THREE MEN AND A BOY IN A BED

In mid-June, I again stayed overnight with Tim and his family. I spent the afternoon and evening at the home with the combined families: Tim; his wife, Linda; Stuart, their seven-year-old son; and Tim's spiritual brother, Paul, and his two biological sons. I knew I would be sleeping with Paul that night because Paul had a queen- or king-size bed, and everyone else had their own room.

I was looking forward to sleeping with this extremely attractive man. I only wondered whether I would be able to cuddle with him like I cuddled with Tim. I doubted it given that he didn't have any homosexual feelings of which I was aware—Tim said he was straight—and he had a girlfriend, Kimberly, and the boys. Also, he didn't strike me as a touchy-feely kind of person. He was kind to me but didn't come off as trying extra hard to be close. He seemed like a fairly typical male to me, indifferent and self-satisfied, goal-oriented rather than relationship-oriented, and cockily confident.

I had specific hopes for that evening. I hoped I would be able to touch Paul like I touched Tim. I hoped he would touch me like Tim touched me, although I didn't expect it was likely. I also hoped to see him nude. He had a master bathroom off his bedroom, and perhaps he might leave the door open while he showered or prepared for bed, or maybe he would even sleep nude.

It was getting late, and Tim and Paul were still up. I announced I was going to bed and said goodnight to everyone. Tim, knowing how much I wanted to be touched, assured me he would come in and say goodnight in a few minutes. After a while, he came in, and we held each other and caressed for awhile. He said goodnight and went back into the living room with Paul.

I lay in bed alone, staring at the ceiling and waiting. But Paul didn't come. It seemed like twenty or thirty minutes had passed when I quietly walked into the kitchen, where I could get a view of the living room. Tim was lying on the couch, his shirt open, and Paul was rubbing his stomach while Tim quietly giggled, sounding like a child making some expression of pleasure. I knew that Tim's child alter egos must be out, and Paul, as his spiritual brother, was providing physical and emotional comfort like Tim provided for me. It bothered me to see Tim behaving like this, and I thought it must be pretty weird for Paul as well. I could see how needy Tim was and how dependent he was on Paul, and this scared me because I depended on him to be a mature, strong, and wise father. I returned quietly to Paul's room.

After a long time, Paul came into the room. I was still awake. Paul used the bathroom and crawled into bed wearing a T-shirt and underwear. I never got to see him nude. After we lay there silently for a while, I asked Paul whether it would be okay if I leaned against him. He mumbled yes. I scooted up next to him and leaned my back against his side. I tried to engage him in conversation, and he answered my questions, but he didn't initiate any of his own. I still hoped I could touch him more or he would touch me, but it didn't happen. I lay there wide awake, soaking in his masculinity while he seemed to be falling asleep oblivious to my hopes.

After a while, I heard someone come into the room. It was Tim. In a small, weak, almost whiny, childlike voice, I heard my spiritual dad say to Paul, "Paul, I can't sleep. Can I get in bed with you?" Paul, half-asleep, said yes, and Tim crawled over the top of him and placed himself between Paul and me. In his normal, but sleepy voice, he said, "Hi, son," and gave me a quick squeeze to assure me of his presence. It was as if Tim were simultaneously two people, a needy little boy with his spiritual brother, Paul, and a father to me. I began massaging Tim, who seemed conflicted between getting his emotional needs met from Paul and making sure he was being a father to me. We lay there together for quite a while before I heard someone else enter the room.

It was seven-year-old Stuart. Now, with a sincere child's voice, Stuart said, "Daddy, I can't sleep. Can I sleep with you?" Stuart climbed in between Paul and Tim, and now three men and a boy shared this giant bed. I lay there in the dark silence and thought, *What the hell am I doing here? This is the craziest situation in the world. I should get out of bed, get dressed, drive home right now, and leave this family situation forever. This is just too weird. I can't believe this is happening.* I was close to doing it, but I couldn't. I was too afraid. I needed Tim. I needed his attention and his affection. I couldn't walk away from this relationship, no matter how crazy it was.

Why couldn't I walk away from the relationship at that point? What was keeping me dependent on this man I called father? I was still convinced that this level of intimacy with a man, this almost unlimited physical and emotional availability, was the only thing that would heal my chronic feelings of loneliness and emptiness. Nothing other than physical and emotional contact with men had ever given me solace and comfort from my anxiety.

After a short while, Tim took Stuart back to his room, and I don't know where Tim slept the rest of the night, but he didn't return to sleep with Paul and me. Most likely, he returned to his wife. Fitfully, I tossed and turned and got only a few hours of sleep. I felt tormented with anxiety over the insanity of my situation. How could I possibly feel safe with a man who acted like a little boy to get his "tummy" rubbed from a hunk he called his spiritual brother? How could such a man take care of me and be deserving of being called Dad? I felt trapped in a relationship more complicated than I ever thought it could be.

29

It's Not Working

During the summer of 1998, my issues had not been resolved by my therapeutic and familial experiences with Tim Neumann. In spite of all the therapy hours and time spent with him alone and with his family, I still felt overwhelming levels of loneliness, fear, and anxiety and was often worried about our relationship. I had all the same fears and anxieties in my relationship with my friend and supervisor Todd Evans, as well. I was consolable for short periods of time, but my anxiety always returned.

My relationship with Veronica was dependable and steady as a good friendship, but it lacked the emotional and sexual passion that a romantic relationship would typically have. I didn't let that bother me since I was convinced that obeying God was all that mattered, and if God wanted me to find a mate, he would make it happen. Despite our relationship's lack of passion, I brought up the subject of marriage several times. Each time, Veronica wisely said that neither of us was ready for such a thing, and although she wasn't ruling it out, it was too early to be seriously considering it. I tried to be helpful around her house, doing yard work for her, for example. She cooked me exceptional meals.

I wanted to see Dr. Ashman again. I trusted this man more than anyone. I wanted to explore my issues with him, not only the original ones with which I had entered counseling six months earlier, but also the new ones associated with my confusing relationship with Tim. My time spent with Tim was free at this point, but Dr. Ashman charged $90 a session.

During the time of the molestation accusation, Kim Adams had told me the agency would pay for up to nine sessions with Dr. Ashman. Though the issue was now resolved, I asked if I might still accept the offer. She agreed. On July 30, I met with Dr. Ashman, the man I considered my spiritual granddad, although he never acknowledged the title and there were plenty of opportunities to do so. In fact, one day I referred to him as Tim's "spiritual dad," and he corrected me by saying, "Tim has called me that," implying the title might be in Tim's mind only.

In the next two and a half months, I poured out my thoughts and feelings to Dr. Ashman, everything from the accusation of James Evans to my "spiritual adoption" by Tim to chronic feelings of emptiness and anxiety and my lifelong desire for intimacy with men. Every time I left Dr. Ashman's office, I felt better. I felt understood, appreciated, respected, and more capable of handling my own life.

On Thursday, August 20, I cried most of the way to Dr. Ashman's office. That morning, I felt particularly estranged from my friend Todd Evans, so much so that I had avoided putting my hand on his back during the morning meeting out of fear and anger. Todd was very good to me. He repeatedly affirmed our friendship and demonstrated patience with my neediness and anxiety. He even went so far as to let me lean against him on a couch in my office when I was terribly upset. In contrast to Tim, Todd had never suggested in the slightest way that he was attracted to me physically or sexually. If anything, Todd was uncomfortable with my request for physical closeness and reminded me I wasn't a child anymore and couldn't expect people to treat me like one. He said holding each other was something husbands and wives did, not adult male friends. As we parted that morning, I had tears in my eyes, and our hands touched briefly as I left, but I dare say more love was conveyed in this simple gesture than in hours of caressing with Tim.

On my way to Dr. Ashman's office, I told God how lonely I was. I still couldn't feel close to Tim, and I couldn't feel close to Todd either. That morning, I took a book with me titled *Desires in Conflict*, by Joe Dallas (1991). I read a short entry to Dr. Ashman:

Homosexuality is not a "heaven or hell" issue. Nobody goes to heaven because they are heterosexual; nobody goes to hell because they are homosexual ... The question for the Christian, then, isn't whether or not his struggles will doom him to hell (they won't), but rather how he can best overcome his struggles because, as a child of God, he has been born to higher purposes ... If you're a child of God, you're not going to hell regardless of your struggles or your sin. Don't "go straight" to try to become a child of God; rather, abandon sin because you already are a child of God. Homosexuality, then, sends no one to hell. (pp. 40, 41)

I looked up at Dr. Ashman and asked whether he agreed with this. He said he did. I felt like a free man. I wasn't ready to decide to be gay, but I could give up my fear of hell over it.

That morning, Dr. Ashman asked me, "How can God love your mom?" I thought about how God might see my mother in such a way that he felt love and compassion and forgiveness for her. I had held resentment toward her all those years and linked so many of my difficulties back to our bitter relationship. I blamed her for my emotional problems and my resentment toward women.

Dr. Ashman said I feared God rejecting me because I rejected myself and my mother. I rejected everything about her and everything about myself that resembled her, including such things as femininity, emotional neediness, and emotional instability. He said, "It's obvious why you don't want a woman in your life when the woman represents all the parts of yourself you rejected." He said I was "disconnected" from myself, and my longing for closeness with men was really my need to be close to myself. He suggested I stop rejecting parts of myself I perceive to be evil or dangerous and instead embrace all of me. I don't know whether he was suggesting I accept myself as gay. I doubt it because he and Tim's therapeutic goal was to help gay men go straight, but he definitely gave me permission to stop hating myself and start loving and trusting myself.

I gave him a couple examples of times I felt free. I told him I enjoyed hiking nude in the national forest above my home. I told him I enjoyed not worrying about getting an erection in the university showers where I swam. I contrasted the freedom I felt in these situations with the fear and anxiety I experienced over obsessive-compulsive symptoms such as the need to use toilet paper when opening a doorknob. Most of my tears in the office that day were ones of relief and joy rather than sadness, and certainly not fear. Dr. Ashman gave me permission to stop worrying about going to hell and to embrace the parts of myself I feared and rejected and to extend that love and compassion to my mother as well.

In the two months ahead, I grew closer emotionally to Dr. Ashman without ever touching him than I had in the months prior with Tim. This is why therapists are forbidden to have physical relationships with their clients. There are reasons for therapeutic boundaries and professional guidelines. They protect both clients and therapists alike.

During this same time period, I continued to meet with Tim. Our time was spent holding each other with a minimal amount of talking and almost no analysis at all. As before, he usually fell asleep. I grew bored and angry and more and more resentful.

My meetings with Dr. Ashman were productive and encouraging. Each week, I felt stronger and more independent and less needy for Tim. I also accepted myself more as a sexual person and a powerful person able to take care of myself. I shared my complaints and disappointments in Tim with Dr. Ashman.

Feeling more confident, I told Tim that I didn't trust him, I felt used, and I didn't feel safe. On September 14, I feared that perhaps I had pushed him too far and apologetically wrote,

> I feel like I don't do a very good job of honoring you ... I tell you what's on my mind. I try not to hide my thoughts ... Sometimes I think the more I say the more I hurt your feelings in some way. I hope not because I love you and I don't want to make you feel unhappy in any way ... I'm really sorry when I make you feel badly or disappoint you with my pestering questions or lack of trust. I don't know if I would put up with me if I was you, but I trust you are able to handle me because ... you're committed to your children.

October 22 was my ninth appointment with Dr. Ashman. He said if I wanted to speak with him in the future, he would be glad to meet with me as needed. On November 11, Tim and I planned to go to Disneyland, just the two of us, but he canceled at the last minute because he was sick. We rescheduled for December 16.

Our communication between sessions was minimal. Our time in his office was unsatisfying and emotionally and intellectually stagnant. Although I was growing tired of the holding, I was also glad to not feel so needy and dependent on him. I also felt less arousal, even very little at times. I did feel more *solid* inside, hugged even when I wasn't being held, but it is difficult to know to what degree these observations were accurate because I wanted so much to see progress. Also, it is difficult to know how much of these changes were the result of my relationship with Tim and how much were the result of my counseling sessions with Dr. Ashman.

As December 16 approached, I looked forward to our trip to Disneyland but had a nagging fear Tim might cancel again. We planned to leave at 10:00 in the morning and spend the whole day together. The day before, Tim canceled. This time I was not just disappointed. I was angry. I felt betrayed. I thought of Tim as a flake. I called Dr. Ashman and asked if I could meet with him immediately.

I had grown to think of Tim as undependable, emotionally needy himself, and someone I did not want to continue being dependent on. I resented him at that moment more than I needed him. I met with Dr. Ashman for two days in a row and talked through everything that had transpired between Tim and me from the beginning. We had reached a point where our relationship was little more than holding each other in his office while he fell asleep. I didn't feel good about what we had, and I wanted to get out of the relationship, at least for several months, to see how I felt about him.

Dr. Ashman agreed this would be a wise thing to do. I sensed in him a relief at the thought of Tim and me going our separate ways. Though he never told me so, I am sure he was deeply concerned about the things that had happened between Tim and me and had warned Tim that his license and practice were in danger. He was also likely concerned for his own reputation as Tim's supervisor and for the reputation and future of his counseling center.

That night, I wrote a letter to Tim. I didn't want to hurt him. I was grateful for what he had provided for me, and although disappointed in the final outcome, I was confident this was all part of God's will.

December 17, 1998

Dear Dad,

I need to communicate something really important to you. My disappointment over the Disneyland thing is a small part of what I've been feeling for awhile. I think that because of your adopting me, your consistent care for my emotional well-being, your willingness to spend time with me every week, at times more than once a week, that I have outgrown our current relationship. I have not been looking to you in the same way for the leadership role that you have been in. I don't feel like you're taking me farther than I am, that we are stagnating. I don't have the desire to keep getting together like we have been. I need to go away now, to wait on God to find out what God wants us to be to each other. I'm thinking that I should stay away for about three months to have time to think, to pray, to hear from God's heart again. What does he want for us now?

I've been confident, and still am confident, that he brought us together, that it was good and right that I called you Dad and you called me Son. I believe that I have changed dramatically in the short time we have been in this relationship. As you know, I no longer have been experiencing the depression cycles I used to go through. I feel handsome. I feel masculine. I feel "solid" inside. I am so grateful to God and to you for helping me discover these things in myself. You helped bring them out in me. You affirmed me. You let me be a child. You let me cry and say "scary" things. You didn't reject me. You kept your word that you wouldn't reject me. You showed authentic sadness at my pain. You loved me even when there was a chance in your mind that I might be a perpetrator.

I am so grateful for your love for me. Thank you, thank you, thank you. But I need to go away from you for awhile now as I've said. Will you pray also for what God wants us to be to each other? There was a time when all I wanted was to be "little" and for you to be my "Daddy." I wanted to crawl up inside of you and be safe. I don't want that anymore, perhaps because I don't think that I need that anymore. I really am grateful, Dad, and I don't know what God holds for the future, but I'm being real and authentic right now by separating for a time. Thank you for understanding.

You really aren't just a warm body to me anymore. I love you, Tim Neumann.

Love,

Brian

CC: Dr. Bill Ashman

Five days later, on a Tuesday, Tim wrote back.

22 Dec. 98

Dear Brian,

Thank you for your letter. That was very thoughtful of you. I really don't want to comment or respond to what you've said, because I don't want to argue with or minimize anything you're feeling. Once again, I am very sorry I had to cancel our trip to Disneyland on such short notice. I would be upset too if I were you. As to your decision to "take some time off" from me, I respect your decision and want you to do what you feel is necessary to take care of yourself.

This will be a very different Christmas for us and others in the family. Susan has separated from her husband and is staying with us temporarily. It is "cozy," but we all feel it's right. In the midst of all of this—God is God—and I am grateful! I love you, son.

Dad

In mid-January 1999, Tim contacted our mission agency and requested a meeting with two of our staff members: Todd Evans, my close friend and immediate supervisor, and Jia Barnes, a licensed mental health therapist who also worked for our agency and with whom I had shared many personal details about my relationship with Tim. Jia had met privately with Dr. Ashman at least once at her request and with my permission. Tim initiated this meeting because he was required to do so by the team of therapists at Christ's Counseling Center.

Todd and Jia agreed to meet with him on Saturday, January 30, 1999.

In anticipation of their meeting, I provided them with detailed information about our relationship. It appeared that this was going to be Tim's opportunity to give his side of the story. According to Todd, Tim spent most of the time defending himself and suggesting I might have a serious mental disorder called borderline personality disorder. He also said he expected I would turn him into the Board of Behavioral Sciences. Other than this, I wasn't told anything else, and I didn't ask questions. From my point of view, I was done worrying about Tim.

Four months went by before I wrote a letter to Tim permanently ending our relationship. When I separated from him in December, I felt free for the first time in many months. I was able to think clearly again and was free to work on my own issues without the added confusion of pretending to be a little boy and calling anyone "father" other than my own biological dad, who deserved the title. I grew to appreciate my own dad much more and also my male friends at the mission agency.

On April 15, 1999, I explained to Tim in a letter that I believed God's role for him in my life had been a temporary one and that I had struggled with calling him Dad, the title always feeling foreign, no matter how much I had wanted it to be true at the time. I compared his role to that of a foster parent, temporarily caring for me, but for the purpose of returning me to my own parents. I asked him to convey my appreciation to each of the members of his biological and spiritual family and suggested that if he felt the need to contact me, he please do so through a letter. I did not want him to contact me directly. I sent a copy of the letter to Dr. Ashman as well.

30

WORKING WITH A FEMALE THERAPIST

A month later, I was ready to find another therapist and work on the issues that had come up as a result of my spiritual adoption experience with Tim as well as the issues that had brought me to him in the first place. On Tuesday, May 25, 1999, I interviewed Patricia "Pat" Nevett, a licensed therapist, MFCC, in Van Nuys. She had graduated from Fuller Theological Seminary, and I liked her because she seemed nurturing. She had raised three boys and impressed me with her gentle spirit and calm wisdom. Pat was a kind, caring woman about my mother's age, perhaps a little older. On June 3, we had our first official session.

As I relayed my experiences with Tim, Pat expressed her disapproval. Though she didn't tell me what to do, she said she would wholeheartedly support me if I decided to report Tim to the Board of Behavioral Sciences in Sacramento. I told her I was not interested in hurting him in any way, but I was also concerned about him perhaps repeating the pattern with others, and this thought bothered me very much.

As in former counseling settings, I began telling my story from earliest childhood. With the retelling, I felt deep sadness and sobbed with emotion. This level of emotion and intensity during our sessions continued for months. At times I wondered if I would ever stop crying. Pat and I were beginning a professional relationship that lasted nearly a year and a half.

In June 1999, I was still living out the same themes of loneliness and fear of rejection and an inability to feel close to my male friends. No matter how many times they said they loved me or gave me a pat on the back or let me rest my hand on their backs or gave me a hug, I could not feel close enough. I felt like my body was wrapped in cellophane that kept any physical contact from penetrating. Demonstrations of love couldn't stick. The holes in the bottom of the love bucket were still there, and I now looked to Pat to try to help me understand what was going on with me.

The friend who continued to suffer the most because of my insecurities and neediness was Todd. I repeatedly interpreted his behavior as rejection, even after finding out time and again that I had misread his actions. I judged him to be distant, and I found myself falling apart emotionally in order to justify asking for his attention. I wanted to be held by him, but I knew he didn't feel comfortable holding me, especially after the disaster with Tim.

I reminded myself of the things I had learned from Dr. Ashman. I needed to love myself and be the man I was seeking. I needed to be the man I wanted to lean against. I needed to be the man I wanted to hold me. For whatever reason, and I still don't understand it, I wept as I thought about leaning against my own chest. I needed to become my own best friend.

31

TIME TO FILE A COMPLAINT

In early June 1999, I decided I needed to report my therapeutic experience with Tim Neumann to the Board of Behavioral Sciences (BBS) in Sacramento. It had been a month and a half since I had written my final letter ending my relationship with Tim and five and a half months since I had last seen him. Obviously, I was not anxious to report him to the BBS. It was not up to me to decide whether our relationship was appropriate or whether they would take his license or monitor him or whatever else. It was only my responsibility to let them know what had happened. I knew Tim was working on a book about spiritual adoption, and I knew that if I someday attended a mental health workshop, and he was the speaker and he talked about how wonderful spiritual adoption was, I would be angry. I did not want to see him repeat the experience he had with me with someone else. I could not know what he would or wouldn't do, but as long as I carried out my responsibility to report what had happened, I was confident it would be handled well.

I have been asked again and again why I wasn't angry earlier, far earlier, in our relationship. I don't see the point of being angry. I suppose getting angry might have removed me from the relationship earlier, but I'm still not angry. I believe Tim did the best he could with what he had. I don't believe Tim purposefully took advantage of me or sought to use me for his own emotional or sexual purposes. I believe he had good intentions from the beginning and throughout our relationship. I don't think he consciously thought to do anything harmful to me. I think his professional judgment was poor, and

I think his own emotional and sexual conflicts clouded his ability to make good decisions.

I called the Board of Behavioral Sciences in Sacramento, and they asked me to complete a Consumer Complaint Form. On Monday, June 14, I completed it along with a Release of Information for Complaints form authorizing Dr. Bill Ashman to discuss everything about me with the BBS.

The day after I completed the Consumer Complaint Form, I met with Pat for our second counseling appointment. I shared with her my anxieties and fears associated with reporting my former relationship with Tim to the BBS. I knew that Tim would be disappointed and angry about my decision and that he could lose his license. Pat assured me that I was doing the right thing and that any decisions the board made were up to them, not me. If he were to lose his license, it would not be because of my turning him in, but because of his behavior as a therapist.

Within a few days, I received a letter informing me that the BBS was starting an investigation. A week later, I received another letter, this time asking for proof of my therapeutic relationship with Tim. They suggested canceled checks. I had to complete a second Release of Information for Complaints form, giving the BBS permission to approach Tim regarding my complaint. I sent a cover letter to the enforcement analyst, in which I explained,

> I have come to believe that I was taken advantage of by a therapist who believed sincerely that what he was doing was good and helpful, but whose own psychological problems prevented him from seeing the damage he was doing to someone who already was vulnerable sexually and emotionally. Just as I was taken advantage of sexually by my fourteen-year-old uncle as a nine-year-old boy, I believe that Tim also took advantage of me sexually and emotionally. In both cases, an older trusted "adult" took advantage of the emotional neediness of a "child."
>
> I think this aspect of me feeling "like a child" is well documented through my writings during that time period, my conversations with Dr. Bill Ashman, conversations with another licensed MFCC therapist named Jia Baines, conversations with my friends, and my conversations with Tim Neumann himself.

Ultimately, the reason I am filing this report is because I do not want Tim Neumann to repeat this pattern of "healing" with others. I believe that he did what he did with the intention of being helpful. However, I think that he has demonstrated himself to be a poor therapist with little concept of healthy boundaries and enough psychological confusion himself to cloud the objectivity needed to help others.

On July 1, I received another letter informing me that my complaint had been referred to the Department of Consumer Affairs, Division of Investigation, and I should anticipate being contacted by an investigator. He soon came to my office and interviewed me there. The interview was what I expected: straight to the point, with questions about dates, times, actions, and so on. Everything was well documented in my folder titled "May I Call You Dad?" As mentioned earlier, I had intended to use this folder and its contents to document a successful spiritual adoption that would lead to my transformation from gay to straight. Unfortunately, it ended up serving a different purpose.

32

Heat of Summer

I survived the accusation of James Evans. I survived the confusion of my relationship with Tim Neumann. I found a therapist with whom I felt safe and comfortable. I was coming up on my five-year anniversary of joining the mission agency where I lived and worked. I was considering asking for a month off. I was beginning to believe that I could learn to relax, that God loved me without expectation or judgment, and that I was secure in his love.

My parents wanted to visit me at the end of July. I worried how I might entertain them while they were here, but my mom said again and again on the phone, "Brian, your dad and I are coming to see *you*. We don't need to be entertained." She meant it. They were looking forward to spending time with me.

I looked forward to seeing them too, especially to show them where I lived and worked, but I also felt guilty because I feared I didn't love them like they loved me. Maybe I wasn't capable of loving them. After all, I had spent the majority of my life blaming them, especially my mother, for my emotional difficulties. I had rehearsed the "tragic" story of my childhood hundreds of times. I was in therapy seemingly because of them, and then I listened to the heartfelt, loving words of my mom, who wanted the best for me, wished she could give me the world, and insisted my company was all she and my dad wanted; that alone motivated them to travel five hundred miles to see me.

The day before my parents flew home, at my request, we met together with Pat, my new therapist. My parents liked her, and we had a good conversation—

nothing dramatic or emotional, but a friendly, comfortable conversation. Prior to their meeting, I had described my mom to Pat as domineering. After my parents were gone, she told me that although my father may be quiet, he was very much in control. She did not see the gross imbalance of power I had described.

I was grateful to my parents for their willingness to meet with her. I had hoped that Pat would dig deep into my parents' personalities and my many complaints would be substantiated, but she didn't, and they weren't, and most importantly, they didn't need to be. My father shared with Pat his observation that I had suffered from anxiety and depression since childhood, and exercise seemed to help. He suspected much of my trouble might be the result of some sort of chemical or biological problem.

Soon after this meeting, Pat asked me to read a book on obsessive-compulsive disorder. She also suspected that much of my emotional turmoil was the result of my biology. After reading the book, I feared Pat was minimizing the sadness and loneliness I felt by suggesting, "Oh, that's just your OCD." I admitted I had suffered as a child with the pain described by the people in this book, but I no longer did as an adult. I didn't want to explain away the depth of my needs with a simple diagnosis. It would be eight more months of misery before I finally came to accept that I had a chemically based problem.

Through the end of March 2000, I continued to obsess on my feelings of loneliness and sadness. One morning, I went to Todd's office to ask him what he was working on. What I really wanted was for him to come to my office, sit beside me on the couch, let me lay my head on him, stroke my hair or massage my back, and say something like, "I'm really sorry it hurts inside." That would be so comforting. I felt sad thinking about it because I didn't want him to be grossed out and think, "I don't want to touch him like that! I'm not gay! He's just being gay and trying to get me to be sexual with him in disguise!" I hated to think about the possibility of him thinking this of me. I walked silently back to my office.

Todd called me on the phone and asked whether I was okay. I lied and said yes. I wished he knew my thoughts. I wished it was safe to tell him everything. It made me sad to consider the possibility that perhaps it had been safe all along, but he had never let me know, and I could never ask. Could he really let me be that close to him? I wanted that so badly.

I considered the possibility that these feelings might be the result of OCD. It hurt too much to be so easily explained. I thought about how Tim had met some of my needs, but our relationship felt sullied. I didn't want closeness with Todd to feel that way. That would depend on him, whether he could be physically and emotionally close to me without feeling uncomfortable. Could he be affectionate and not be afraid of me and my homosexual feelings and the intensity of my sadness and loneliness?

I'm confident it was not sex I wanted from Todd or Tim. I realize now how similarly the situation played out between these father figures and me at thirty-four and my own biological father and me at eight and nine and ten. As a child, I wanted desperately to be physically comforted by my father, but I feared he would be uncomfortable holding me, maybe even find me repulsive. I feared his physical contact because I didn't want him to feel dirty holding me like I felt being held by my uncle. Being held already had been contaminated, and I feared my dad would feel repulsion holding me, even though this was what I wanted more than anything in the world.

Todd, without ever rejecting me, said that he was uncomfortable with my neediness and that his primary relationships were with his wife and his son. He insisted he didn't feel "dirty" holding me but also didn't think he could be what I needed. He felt I was prolonging my problem by seeking closeness with men when I should be finding this sort of comfort from a woman.

In late September, I wrote out my feelings again and this time focused more on my fear of Todd. I kept asking myself, "Why am I afraid of him? Why do I feel like crying whenever I think of him?" My answer was that my internal state was one of chronic feelings of guilt and fear, including fear of being evil. These feelings were the exact ones I had experienced when I was having sex with my uncle and then with the neighbor boys. I feared my father's rejection back then, and I still feared the rejection of father figures at this point in my life. In each case, I gave them the power to absolve me, to declare me clean, to tell me I was lovable, and to make me feel safe. To be refused this comfort was to be left feeling utterly alone and trapped in my anxiety. Because the feelings of desperation traveled from man to man, I knew that not one of these men was the problem or the solution to my anxiety. I was putting the pieces together but still lacked the critical piece of OCD.

33

NATURE SPEAKS AGAIN

I asked for a month off from my work. I took two weeks to travel to Colorado, where I stayed in a lodge and hiked during the day in the mountains of Grand Mesa National Forest, at an elevation between 10,000 and 11,000 feet. Daily, I walked along the Crag Crest Trail, soaking in the breathtaking views of thirty or more lakes, clear blue skies, flitting butterflies, and the endless expanse of aspen-laden forest, as far as I could see in any direction. This was Colors Sunday Week, and the leaves were at the pinnacle of their varied colors—red, amber, purple, yellow, orange, and gold.

I always think clearly in nature, and it was in this setting that light began to break through the dark clouds of my thinking, and yet I rejected the very insights as they came. On September 29, 1999, I wrote,

> It is Wednesday night, only one and a half days left before returning home. Today was a bit disappointing as I hiked Crag Crest again. Most of my time was spent thinking about sex, intimacy, homosexuality, nudity, and commitment to a life partner, male or female. These consuming thoughts seem to demean the beauty of the creation. I grieve over my own feelings of inadequacy in light of God's goodness and my own sinful propensities. I feel so weak emotionally and sexually.
>
> Why don't I long for a woman? I have begun to wonder whether sexual feelings, in general, attach themselves to whatever stimulates them? I feel as if I am fighting against myself. I know there are

other men out here also who feel hopeless tonight, lonely, and sad. Some of them, perhaps one in particular, I would feel very drawn to. I would invite him to stay here with me in this condo and we would share my bed. I would sleep nude as I always do. He can sleep however he wants to. I would be there to hold him if he wants to be held. We could lean against each other through the night if he wants to. Otherwise I'm fine to sleep alone. I have slept alone most of my life. I can do so another night.

I am so sorry God for my longings which are at odds with your Bible. I hope your Bible is wrong or I hope you persevere in conforming me to your Son's image and likeness, even if it's not my belief or desire of who I am or want to be. I would like to be straight if it were as real to me as homosexuality is to me right now. God, if you could heal my heart to where I would desire a woman like I desire a man, I would be happy. I can't fake attraction and desire. It must be real.

As I read my words in the present, I am grieved at the insane level of guilt, shame, and fear I was experiencing at that time. I see how clearly I wanted intimacy with a man and not a woman, and the only obstacle to the fulfillment of my desires was my religious convictions at the time. All of it, I find disturbing, but the line that stands out to me the most is this: "These consuming thoughts seem to demean the beauty of the creation." No, no, no, I say today. Instead, sex, intimacy, homosexuality, nudity, and commitment to a life partner, male or female, exemplify the beauty of the creation. They don't demean it.

Though I didn't come close to the freedom I have today, I made huge strides of growth in those inspiring mountains of Colorado. I came home to California with a commitment to authenticity. I was not going to run away from who I was and hide myself from others. I was going to keep alive the powerful self I experienced along the heights of those mountain crests. Even if it cost me my job, I was not going to die emotionally in Southern California.

34

A Cold Winter

On December 20, the Board of Behavioral Sciences alerted me that my complaint against Tim Neumann had "been referred to the Office of the Attorney General for review and possible initiation of disciplinary action." They also told me to not expect a quick decision; both the seriousness of the situation and the caseload of the attorney general's office made this process a lengthy one.

Winter has always been a difficult time of year for me. My favorite seasons are spring and summer. I'm convinced sunlight plays an important role in my emotional life. In mid-February 2000, my fears became unbearable. I cried daily and could barely carry on with my work. I feared the thought of total isolation, a hell of sorts where no one else existed, where it was silent, gross, and evil. I feared the loss of Todd in my life. I feared that my neediness and emotional instability would frighten him away. I feared the loss of my male friends and my parents and God. I thought about Tim and how, even as physically available as he had made himself to me, it wasn't enough. I hoped the only reason it hadn't been enough was that he had brought his own sexual and emotional conflicts into it. I still wanted someone like Todd to be that perfect father figure who would assure me life was safe.

So many people during this time showed me love, and yet I found their expressions of love to be painful. Many times I tried to figure out why love hurt so much. Perhaps I couldn't accept their love because I couldn't stand the thought of them eventually rejecting me. I was sure that everyone would eventually say, "Get away from me. I hate you. You are evil. You are dirty.

You are nasty. You make me feel gross." Then they would leave me. I didn't think anyone could live up to the level of my desperate feelings. Certainly they would hate me if they knew how much I needed them. I was convinced that my needing someone too much would make them go away. It would make them not want to be around me.

One afternoon, at one of the lowest points of my experience, I asked Todd whether he would allow me to sit beside him and read parts of a book I found insightful. He said yes, and we sat together. I leaned against him, opened up my book, and began to read. For the next fifteen or twenty minutes, I felt safe, loved, accepted, and hopeful.

Todd returned to his office, and my cycle of fear returned. Perhaps he might finally be pushed over the edge of his patience with my desperation and never let me lean against him again. Perhaps he might fear being sexually attracted to me and therefore couldn't ever touch me again. Perhaps he might touch me in a sexual way and pervert this wonderful feeling of innocence.

In anticipation of my next counseling appointment with Pat, I asked Todd to write down a few ideas of what he thought she and I should be discussing. He wrote, "The thing that came up recently was this area of obsession in the OCD picture—it would be good to examine why you are so focused on one person, thinking about me, what am I doing, what am I thinking, and so on. The other important thing you brought up Tuesday was the idea of believing you are evil. This is not true of course, but it seems to have a powerful grip on you, and renders you helpless at times."

I filled pages and pages of my journal with further thoughts and fears about Todd. I wanted intimacy, but I didn't know how to be close. I couldn't get close enough to people to be satisfied or satiated. The hugs of my friends and family could not reach me. When they hugged me or told me they loved me, it didn't feel real. As if I was a prisoner behind a plate glass window, they visited me and put their faces up to the glass and said, "I love you. I love you." The more they said it, the worse it hurt because I could not touch them, and they could not touch me.

By late February, I knew I needed serious help, maybe even medical help. I cried for hours each day. My journaling was repetitious and exhaustive, clearly the ranting of a man tormented by my incessant thoughts. I wanted to either find relief or die. I imagined myself driving in the winding mountains above my home and failing to make a turn, falling to my death hundreds of feet below. I contacted a psychiatrist, Dr. Marc Graff, with whom I had developed a relationship exactly three years earlier.

In February 1997, a full year before any of the events related in this book, I had met with him at the insistence of a therapist named Marian Waters, whose counsel I had sought in relation to my having homosexual feelings. I had thought working with a woman might be helpful since I had such a poor relationship with my mother. I was looking to Ms. Waters to take the role of a caring, loving mother. After listening to my early childhood experiences, she said she wanted me to first see Dr. Graff.

When we met, after a lengthy interview, he diagnosed me with obsessive-compulsive disorder (OCD) as a child, as noted earlier, but said I did not meet the criteria for it as an adult. With a chuckle, he told me Marian Waters had sent me to him was because she was concerned I might be psychotic, given the bizarre fears I'd had as a child. Although I didn't meet the criteria for adult diagnosis, he said I could consider taking a minimal amount of medication to minimize the anxiety and depression from which I was suffering. I decided not to take the medication because I didn't want to depend on a chemical to make me happy.

However, three months later, on May 6, 1997, I called his office and left a message telling him that I had changed my mind about medication and faxed through an explanation: I suspected that many of my behaviors could be seen as evidence of the severe anxiety experienced by people with obsessive-compulsive disorder and my attempts to calm myself down: extreme need for order, inability to remember things, frequent hand washing, fear that my thoughts might have the power to harm someone, thoughts and music getting stuck in my head, extreme concerns about pleasing or offending God, daily masturbation in spite of attempts to resist, excessive exercise, and intense need for physical contact. I continued, "Although I have usually seen my behaviors as what cause me worry and anxiety and depression, I now seriously wonder if they are my attempts to calm myself from a body that is chemically anxious or depressed."

He wrote a prescription for Zoloft, and on May 8, 1997, I bought my first prescription for this medication. I took only a couple pills, changed my mind again, and didn't continue. I was afraid. I also stopped working with Ms. Waters after a few sessions. She was not the warmhearted, motherly, nurturing person I was looking for. She probably saw "codependent" written all over me and decided from day one that wasn't going to happen to her.

So on February 25, 2000, I called Dr. Graff's office and with tears explained my situation to another psychiatrist who was acting on Dr. Graff's behalf because he was on vacation. The doctor wrote in his notes, "Not on meds, diagnosed with OCD by Dr. Graff, is depressed, crying, sees a therapist—non K, complains of molestation by his uncle, has 'desire to be held by a man in order to be soothed,' thought he was gay—but no longer thinks so, many issues, denies suicidal impulses, verbose." The earliest appointment I could get with Dr. Graff was a month away, March 28.

By mid-March, I was as emotionally distressed as when I had made the appointment with Dr. Graff. I cried nearly every day, all day, feeling horribly isolated, alone, afraid, and needy and longing to be held by a man. I wasn't sure how I was going to make it until the twenty-eighth. I went from Todd to Wade to Kevin to Alex and attempted to connect in any way, emotionally or physically, that they were willing. I could barely function in my role as director of a training program at our agency.

35

A New Life

Finally, Tuesday, March 28 arrived. I met with Dr. Graff and told him how I was falling apart on so many levels and felt desperate. I wanted to start medication, specifically Zoloft because I had heard good things about it and he had recommended it in the past. On March 29, I wrote, "I took my first Zoloft pill at 50 mg. in the morning. Looking forward to seeing what results I might have." I have to say that this day, Wednesday, March 29, 2000, was the beginning of the end of a lifetime of debilitating emotional problems. It is with tearful gratitude that I contemplate the impact of 50 milligrams of serotonin on my life and the psychiatrist who prescribed it.

Zoloft is a serotonin selective reuptake inhibitor (SSRI), like other antidepressants such as Prozac, Paxil, Luvox, Celexa, and Lexipro. SSRIs are generally used to treat symptoms of depression and anxiety. They can also be helpful for people suffering from panic attacks, obsessive-compulsive disorder, and other anxiety problems. I was suffering primarily from chronic untreated anxiety and the depression that often accompanies it. Since childhood, my mind had never been quiet. I had never known what it felt like to control my own thoughts. My insatiable craving for affection was my desperate attempt to soothe myself and to quiet my incessant thoughts.

Within two weeks of starting serotonin, I noticed changes. I felt far more relaxed than ever before. It seemed as if everything inside of me slowed down. I didn't feel compelled to exercise every day because of excess nervous energy. I still exercised most days, but not out of compulsion. Although I still hugged my friends, I didn't feel excessively lonely and needy, testing their affection by insisting on hugging them. My digestive system worked better. I had more regular bowel movements.

My sexual drive diminished significantly, which initially I appreciated, but then found bothersome. I wanted to feel sexual pleasure, and my penis felt sluggish, as if there were no sexual nerve receptors working, causing a significant delay in sexual arousal during masturbation. I mentioned this to Dr. Graff, who assured me my sexual desire would likely return over time, which it did.

I felt like a new person. I continued to enjoy my daily hikes in the foothills of San Gabriel, but my mind was quiet. With the help of Zoloft, I enjoyed what other people took for granted. I could choose what I wanted to think about and choose what I didn't want to think about. I was in control of my own mind, and I was choosing to stop obsessing on feelings of neediness and emptiness and the themes I had dwelled on for most of my life.

The most significant change I noticed was the ability to not react to things. On a physical level, my body didn't react unnecessarily to minor distress. For example, before Zoloft, if I was walking down steps and missed the last step, slightly jarring my back, I would fear a reaction, and within minutes my entire back would be tight with anxiety and fear. After Zoloft, if I experienced the same jarring, I would keep moving without concerning myself—there was no reaction to the misstep because there was no need for a reaction. On an emotional level, I found myself able to let things go. I stopped feeling desperate about things. I stopped feeling needy and isolated and afraid. I stopped obsessing on what Todd or any of my other male friends might be thinking or not thinking, feeling or not feeling, about me.

The emotional and spiritual seedpods that had been planted among the fall leaves and aspens of Colorado were now cracking open with new life in the spring. With Pat's help, I was able to see my strengths while not denying my weaknesses. I was able to identify myself as a capable, intelligent, and deep person who wanted to live life to its fullest. I was able to acknowledge that I was intensely sexual and not feel guilty for it.

Within a few weeks of beginning Zoloft, I found myself much more relaxed, focused, calm, thoughtful, and even silly at times with Pat. I thought, *What was I so worried about all those years? What was I so concerned about?*

My chronic anxiety and fear were diminished to the point that they weren't debilitating. The simple absence of emotional pain felt so good.

I enjoyed a new and bold honesty with myself and with Pat. I decided my interest in men's bodies in the showers at the university where I swam was a sexual one and not some deep psychological emptiness resulting from feelings of inadequacy. I relished the thought. It was much easier to understand and felt honest, real, and solid. I thought, *So what?* It wasn't like I could decide not to be interested or aroused anyway. I let go of the worry, and I felt great.

I continued to meet with Pat all spring and into the beginning of summer. That I have so little documentation of those months is testimony to the fact that I stopped obsessing. I had become a compulsive writer in an effort to soothe my constant stream of thoughts, and many of my writings were restatements of how miserably anxious I felt. Now my sessions with Pat moved along quickly and smoothly, and many of the feelings I had formerly felt the need to discuss again and again simply didn't exist. I kept asking myself, "What was I so upset about?" I also began to wonder whether my years of therapy and endless analysis of my chronic feelings of guilt, loneliness, fear, and anxiety had been primarily the result of a chemical imbalance. The things that had bothered me before and consumed hours and hours of therapy—my relationships with my mother, my father, my sisters, and my male friends; my being attracted to men; my impossible desire to find the will of God—didn't bother me anymore. They had little emotional content for me, and I felt solid inside, self-confident, and capable of making decisions and choosing how I wanted to live my life.

36

New Freedoms

My times with Pat were going so well that in July I was able to reduce my sessions with her to twice a month. Because it was summer, I decided to enlarge my nudist experiences to Southern California beaches. I made trips to San Onofre State Beach, where I sunbathed and jogged nude along the shoreline. I made one of my trips with a man named Isaac Damron, whom I had met online. He was gay and a nudist, and I could tell from my communications with him that he was a kind and trustworthy person. All afternoon and into the early evening, we lounged around the shoreline along with a hundred or more other nudists: men, women, and a few children. Isaac had brought a Frisbee, and he and I raced around the sand, laughing and passing it back and forth as we soaked in the beauty of the crashing waves, darting seagulls, each other's innocent and playful vulnerability, and the multitude of similar-minded people around us.

I made a brief reference to my nudist experiences in our mission agency prayer log. In an entry dated July 29, 2000, I wrote, "I enjoy running around naked in the mountains or along a beach." It seems simple now, but at the time it was a major revelation to our religious community. For the first time I shared in a public way my naturist beliefs and actions. Though many people read the entry, only Todd commented. I asked him why he thought no one else responded to my words. He said, "I think most people feel the same way as you, but they don't want to admit it."

Meanwhile, the situation between Tim Neumann and the Board of

Behavioral Sciences continued to unfold. The Office of the Attorney General for the State of California decided to press charges against Tim. Earlier I had been asked whether I would be willing to testify in court if necessary, if the Attorney General decided to pursue charges against Tim. I said I would. Now it was becoming a reality.

When the attorney general's office wrote to me, attached to their cover letter was the formal accusation. In it they charged Tim with "unprofessional conduct" for having "committed multiple acts of sexual abuse and/or sexual misconduct with B.K." A lengthy and detailed list of specifics was enumerated.

After reading through the accusation, I identified three inaccuracies and reported them in a phone call to the deputy attorney general. She said she appreciated my call and took notes on what I said. Later, I wrote her a letter restating what we had discussed.

With each passing month, I felt more joy and freedom to think and to become who I wanted to be. I contemplated the universe with its intricate beauty and infinite design and trusted that I was part of something profound. A yellow crocus opening up in the morning sunshine of spring or a clear black night sky filled with stars or a brook babbling its thoughts to moss-covered rocks as it passed by—these things shouted to me, "God is love. God is incredibly, wonderfully, marvelously, infinitely more awe-inspiring than the human mind or heart can fathom." Life should be fulfilling, meaningful, creative, alive, growing, changing, and enduring.

I found a walk in the mountains more inspiring than a church service, seagulls at the beach more worshipful than choirs, common sinners more pleasant company than apparently less sinful Christians. I felt drawn to the Father's tender voice, saying, "Hush, my child. Hush. Be still and trust that I am God. There is none other. I am your father, and you are my child." I was becoming more comfortable with my own version of Christianity rather than adopting the dogma of others.

37

Marriage, Massage, and Self-Acceptance

In mid-August 2000, my friend Veronica and I made a trip north to visit with my parents. It was their thirty-eighth wedding anniversary, and they had never met her. My parents knew we were considering the possibility of marrying in spite of the difficulties I was having feeling comfortable in the relationship. We were also planning a trip to Dominica so that I could meet her family. She and my parents seemed to be getting along well when my father took me aside privately and said what he had said at other times during my sixteen years of celibacy. "Brian, I think there are people in the world who are gay, and they would probably do better to just accept themselves as gay." Contrary to my earlier arguments and protestations, I thanked him for his thoughts and left it at that.

My mother found me alone and asked, "Brian, are you crazy about this woman? Do you want to hold her and hug her and kiss her and tell her all of your innermost secrets?"

I thought briefly and answered, "No, but I'm sure it will come once we're married."

Without hesitation, my mom said, "That's just crazy. There is no way you should be marrying this woman unless you feel that way about her." To complete her thought, she added, "I don't think you're ever going to love a woman."

I felt hurt and insulted and angry, but what was new? To me, this was just another attack from my mother. I had grown up feeling abused by her, and now she was doing it again. I couldn't see at the time that she was actually trying to help me accept myself as gay and protect me from a major mistake. Instead, I thought, *I've spent sixteen years of effort trying to be heterosexual, and now you say I'm never going to love a woman. What you really mean is that I've never loved you.* Today I see the situation differently. My mom was trying to save me from a mistake, one that would have hurt all of us.

When Veronica and I returned to Southern California, the first thing on my mind was my new gay nudist friend, Isaac. I wanted so much to hang out with him at his home a half-hour away. I called him, and he said to come on over. I arrived and took off my clothes, and we talked about life, about everything. I liked this man so much. After a while, Isaac offered me a massage. I wanted to jump at the thought, but I was afraid. I had been celibate for sixteen years, and I didn't want to break my so-called record. I was proud of the years of self-control.

I told him, "I would like you to give me a massage if you promise not to touch my genitals." He agreed, and I lay back on his bed and immediately got a major erection. Ignoring it, he applied oil to his hands and began to stroke me everywhere with the one exception, as promised. The entire time, I was so aroused I could hardly stand it, but I soaked up the pleasure and touch and intimacy and openness and vulnerability as if I were a dying man soaking up water, all the way to my parched and withered soul.

As I drove home, I thought about how I had been celibate for sixteen years and had done absolutely everything I could think of to be heterosexual and yet still wasn't any more heterosexual than I ever was. If anything, I was more homosexual than ever. I wanted everything I had received from Isaac that night and more.

When I returned to the mission agency, I felt it was necessary to confess my naked massage experience to the founder, Dr. Rudolph Clemens, and the executive director, Leonard Billings. I asked that they meet with me Monday morning, at which time I related everything that had happened and exactly how it had happened. I assured them that I did not intend for it to happen again and that just as I had come to them immediately this time, I would do the same if it ever became necessary again. I asked whether they would be willing to not make this an issue this one time. With kindness and great empathy, they both assured me that they respected and trusted me and appreciated my openness with them.

My massage from Isaac was the fork in the road for my acceptance of myself as gay. I will always be grateful to him for showing me such care while simultaneously respecting my boundaries. I felt more honest, more alive, happier, and more fulfilled than I had in a long time. I was not going to go on living this tormented life of trying to be straight and trying to love Veronica and trying to believe my very nature was sinful. Veronica and I stopped thinking of ourselves as a couple and canceled our trip to Dominica. In my usual pattern, I distanced myself from her for a long time.

I called my dad and asked him whether he still felt the same way about gay people as he had said before. As always, he began by saying he knew the church didn't agree, but he thought gay people should accept themselves for who they are. With trembling lips and shaky voice, I asked him, "Do you think you and Mom could still love me if I accepted myself as gay?"

He responded immediately, "Your mother and I will always do everything we can to support you." I knew that was his way of saying, "We love you."

I said, "I'm not sure what I'm going to do, but I will let you know within the next couple days what I decide."

After hanging up the phone, I knew this was it. I could tell because I felt so free. I was gay. I accepted myself as gay, and I believed God accepted me as gay also. A huge weight was lifted from me. I felt light and airy and relieved and hopeful and happy.

38

END OF THERAPY, MISSION WORK, AND TIM'S LICENSE

I met with Pat three times in August, once in September, and twice in October. October 26, 2000, was my fiftieth and final counseling appointment with her. I felt comfortable enough with who I was that I didn't need to continue our appointments. I knew I would miss her, and I still think about her often. Occasionally, I call her just to say hello. Pat was the epitome of a good therapist. She was calm, encouraging, supportive, and insightful. She identified the core of my issues, my obsessive-compulsive brain chemistry, and my chronic and nearly lifelong struggles with what the French refer to as the doubting disease.

I washed my hands repeatedly because they didn't *feel* clean. I checked doors because they didn't *feel* locked. I checked stovetops because they didn't *feel* off. I checked relationships because I didn't *feel* loved.

Pat was able to normalize my experiences, assure me of my abilities and character, and naturalize my sexuality and desire for intimacy. Without denigrating my faith, she helped me gain a fresh perspective on the unconditional love of God. She helped me accept myself, not just as a gay man, but as a human being. She taught me to be kind to myself, gentle, and loving. She also taught me to be kind to those I spent much of my life blaming for my problems. She was the person I had needed to help me through this difficult and treacherous leg of my journey.

On December 15, 2000, I announced to my financial supporters that I was leaving the mission agency on December 29. I did not tell them the details of what had led me to this decision. Quite simply, I had become too liberal to work there. I hadn't attended church for more than a year despite being officially required to do so. I no longer believed God was wrathful and needed to sacrifice his son to assuage his wrath. I didn't believe the world needed to hear the gospel in order to be saved. I didn't believe homosexuals were inferior to their heterosexual family and friends. I didn't believe Christians should attempt to use their political power to enforce their moral codes. I didn't believe in the traditional concepts of heaven and hell.

What I did believe was there is a loving, intelligent force that fills the universe; that we are all part of a universal plan; that all religions and all people have something of value to offer; that it is the responsibility of each one of us to decide what ideas in life are inspired; that God, being a creator, wants us to be creative; that life truly is a gift; and that if we must err on the side of being foolishly liberal in love or fearfully rigid and dogmatic, we must choose love.

While I was finishing up my last month at the mission agency, Tim Neumann had to decide whether to surrender his marriage and family therapy license or face the charges being brought against him by the Office of the Attorney General for the State of California. He chose to surrender his license and is no longer permitted to practice as a therapist in the State of California.

Copies of all legal documents in the case were sent to me, including a photocopy of Tim's signature, surrendering his license. I felt, and still feel, sad when I think about Tim losing his license. He was trying to do what he believed was best for me. He knew he was taking a great risk in doing what he believed was God's will in spiritually adopting me. As I said earlier, I admire his courage and innovation, while regretting his sexual and emotional weaknesses that tainted our relationship. I don't believe mental health therapists should adopt their clients, and I don't believe they should hold or caress their clients. I think that was a mistake, not only for the obvious legal reasons, but also for the practical ones, including how complicating physical contact can be to a relationship, any kind of relationship, but particularly to a therapeutic one.

39

Resolution

So many difficulties were resolved over the course of three years. In spite of all the changes, or perhaps because of them, I had peace and well-being as never before. The year 2000 was coming to a close. I had survived the worst experience of my adult life, that of being accused of molesting children. I had found quietude in my thoughts and feelings with the aid of a daily supplement of serotonin. I had found peace in my thoughts and feelings through the unconditional support and love of a female therapist who accepted me and encouraged me to discover the richness of who I am. I had found peace in my sexuality while being able to retain my faith in a loving God. I had found joy in hiking in the mountains and running along the shoreline with nothing but the body and smile God gave me. I had found I loved my parents, and they had always loved me.

What shall I make of my relationship with Tim Neumann? How could two well-meaning, devoutly religious men have gotten into such a therapeutic morass? My view is that Tim Neumann needed someone just like me in his life, and I needed someone just like him in mine. As all serendipitous relationships go, we find each other, and we each play the role that the other needs. I hope it is not unkind to believe Tim needed someone like me to challenge his therapeutic methods. I know I needed someone like him to give me everything that I thought could make me whole so that I could realize it wouldn't. Tim gave me what I wanted, but it wasn't enough. Certainly, it was disturbing, confusing, inappropriate, and unprofessional, but its lack of success ultimately led me to the freedom to acknowledge and accept myself as a gay man. If I had not met Tim, I might still be searching for the perfect father figure to satisfy my emptiness and lead me to sexual wholeness.

Regarding Tim Neumann's alleged alter egos, I do not believe he had anything of the sort. I believe he found the terminology a convenient way to behave however he wanted and gain sympathy and collaborators in meeting his sexual and emotional needs. However, I think he believed his own therapeutic explanations for his behavior.

I acknowledge I gained much from my relationship with Tim. I consider him a brave man and a caring father to his biological children as well as his spiritually adopted children. However, I do not regret having turned this case over to the Board of Behavioral Sciences. I believe the potential for greater harm was there, and it was my responsibility to report the circumstances of our relationship. I have no ill feelings toward Tim today. I wish him and his family well, and it is for this reason I have chosen to keep his real name private and will continue to do so.

I do not believe homosexually oriented men and women are so because of a lack of relationship with their same-sex parent. I think it much more probable and common that parents have their own troubles identifying with and bonding with their children who don't see the world exactly as they had planned or perhaps hoped. I do believe that the gay man or lesbian woman needs love, but that is not unique to a particular sexual orientation. I believe love is the foundational essence and sustaining principle of the universe.

40

REPARATIVE THERAPY IN THE NEWS

By the time this book is published, Congresswoman Michele Bachmann and her reparative therapist husband will likely be out of the limelight, but the issue of reparative therapy as an alternative to accepting oneself as gay or lesbian will continue to be debated. Dr. Joseph Nicolosi, quoted multiple times throughout this book, has done an excellent job in making "conversion therapy" or "change therapy" for homosexuals seem legitimate and scientific. I have reread his two most popular books referenced here in an effort to refamiliarize myself with his theories.

What I noticed most about his writings is how repetitious his basic theme is. He says the same thing again and again in a thousand different ways: Male homosexuality is the result of a faulty relationship between a boy and his father. He fails to identify with his father's masculinity and instead identifies with his mother's femininity. Feeling feminine himself, he is drawn to the masculine in an attempt to complete himself.

Nicolosi's ideas are based on a foundational premise that is binary: human beings are created male and female with specific expectations for our behavior to be masculine or feminine. He assumes the normalcy and correctness of traditional ideas of masculinity. Men are meant to be powerful, strong, hard, and initiatory whereas women are meant to be receptive, responsive, soft, and embracing.

When I was in second grade, I was fascinated by the attraction and repulsion of magnets. Each one had a north side and a south side. Proudly, I pointed out to the teacher that this was just like boys and girls. "Boys like girls, and girls like boys, and boys don't like boys, and girls don't like girls." Little did I know that I would soon be a "north" that liked "norths." Perhaps more telling, but unnoticed by me at the time, was that every magnet possessed both potentials.

Nicolosi's explanations for the etiology of homosexuality are similar in that they are simplistic. His recommendations for "healing homosexuality" are basic: Don't do it. Reject all homosexual inclinations as immature attempts to find your own male identity. Reclaim your masculinity by playing sports, form nonsexual relationships with heterosexual men, learn to assert yourself, and practice cultivating romantic relationships with women.

This simple advice, packaged as therapeutic intervention and costing quite a fortune, reminds me of what one well-meaning missionary told me years ago about how to become heterosexual. I was in my late twenties. He was in his sixties. He and I spent much time talking about our shared interests. I told him about my homosexual "struggles," and he wanted to help.

"May I give you some advice?" he asked.

"Of course," I said.

"Well, first of all, when you stand, you should put your feet a little farther apart, like this." He placed his feet solidly on the floor with a wide stance. I imitated him, but he wasn't satisfied. "A little bit more," he prompted. When it was right, he said, "Now, drop your hands to your side and relax. Shake your hands a little bit." I followed his commands. "Now drop your voice a little bit like this." He spoke in a deeper, more resonating tone, which I imitated. I felt silly, but I did what he said because he was serious and I respected him. I dropped my voice and spoke a few words with this more authoritative, "masculine" voice.

"Good. Good," he reassured me. "One other thing," he said. "Don't use the word *precious* or *lovely*. I've noticed you use those words a lot. Heterosexual men don't use those words." I agreed with a nod and wondered about how this might or might not change my desire for men. On my way home, I practiced using my deep voice. Within minutes, I cracked up laughing at myself as I thought about how silly this was.

I believe the reason Joseph Nicolosi's writings are respected among some, mostly deeply religious people is that he does an excellent job of characterizing many of the thoughts and feelings of some homosexual men. What he fails to acknowledge is that there may be commonalities within the brain structures of heterosexual women and homosexual men that will someday explain these similarities. He would never advocate that heterosexual women resist their natural inclinations to be intimate with men. If it is someday found that homosexual men or bisexual men share brain structure and wiring similar to that of heterosexual women, I think it would be foolhardy to expect us to resist our biology in order to satisfy an outdated religious legal code written by human beings thousands of years ago.

Regardless of what we find out about the etiology of homosexuality, the religiously orthodox are not likely to change. After all, they believe they have the word of God. And who can argue with God?

The insanity of the events of this book could not have happened without the religious dogmatism clung to by my bisexual therapist and me. Our beliefs about same-sex love made it impossible for us to live our lives honestly. If we had not believed our desires were sin, we never would have had to play games with words such as "sensual" and "sexual" or call each other "Daddy" and "son" to justify our intimacy. I would not have been in therapy in the first place. I would not have felt guilty for my sexual experiences as a child and felt the need to confess them again and again. I would not have hidden them from my parents. I would not have suffered needlessly for sixteen years of isolation and loneliness because of some religious notion that it's sinful for two men to love each other.

Am I angry? Yes. I never used to think I was, but yes, I am. Religious dogmatism is not just an innocent belief system as legitimate as any other. Whether it's Christianity or Islam or Judaism, or any polytheistic or monotheistic belief system, it is fundamentally flawed because it depends on revelation from a god or gods rather than natural law. Each one is based on someone's claim to divinity, or access to divinity, rather than on natural law available to all of us.

My understanding of love and sexuality and intimacy is evolving. I look forward to discovering what I might believe a year from now, or two or five or ten. I hope to get beyond traditional concepts of male and female, heterosexual and homosexual, masculine and feminine. Every snowflake, every flower, every waterfall, every thing is unique, and so too every human being.

Epilogue

Immediately following the events of this book, I began substitute teaching in the local school district where I lived. The principal encouraged me to apply for a full-time position and hired me for the 2001–2002 school year. I taught second grade for four years before deciding to go into private tutoring. On November 1, 2008, I moved to Northern California to be closer to my parents, sisters, and extended family. I now live in Chico, California, and enjoy our beautiful city of trees, the collegiate community, and most of all my dear family.

I speak on gay, lesbian, bisexual, and transgender issues in classes at California State University, Chico; Butte College; and other public forums whenever invited. I play piano and sing in local churches, for memorial services and weddings, and for seniors in retirement homes. During the summer, I hike and swim naked in our Edenic Upper Bidwell Park and provide a voice for naturist/nudist rights. I live in a city where nude sunbathing and swimming have been a tradition for as long as any of us can remember. I continue to write and look forward to finding meaning in writing and public speaking. Several books are forthcoming.

References

American Psychiatric Association. *Diagnostic and statistical manual of mental disorders.* 4th ed., text rev. Washington, DC: Author, 2000.

Dallas, J. *Desires in conflict: Answering the struggle for sexual identity.* Eugene, OR: Harvest House, 1991.

Nicolosi, J. *Reparative therapy of male homosexuality.* Northvale, NJ: Jason Aronson, 1991.

Nicolosi, J. *Healing homosexuality: Case stories of reparative therapy.* Northvale, NJ: Jason Aronson, 1993.